# PRAISE FOR LOVE AND POWER...

"Garriott expertly jabs at the inflated ego that is Washington while underscoring the necessity for servant-oriented leadership in places where humility and conviction can be counter-cultural."

—**Jesse Byrnes,**
Journalist and Writer, Washington, D.C.

"Chuck Garriott has spent much of his life helping people in positions of power think more carefully about the implications of the gospel for their work and their lives. What a gift, then, for Chuck to share with all of us the lessons he's learned over the years. I believe God will use this book to bless many who desire to steward their influence for the good of others to the glory of God."

—**Michael Wear,**
Author of *Reclaiming Hope: Lessons Learned in the Obama White House* About the Future of Faith in America. Founder, Public Square Strategies

"Garriott is an inspirational thought leader who has brought spiritual guidance to Congressmen, Senators, State leaders and even has written prayers for our presidents. I know that you will enjoy his latest work in *Love and Power*. It is certain to have a profound effect on you."

—**Dan Boren,**
U S House of Representatives, 2005-2013, 2nd District, Oklahoma. President Corporate Development, The Chickasaw Nation

"*Love and Power* sheds light on some of the most important spiritual, political and philosophical mysteries that I have faced and will continue to face: power, leadership, wealth and death.

I am thankful for this in-depth exposition of the message of Christ to the contemporary rulers who do often place "power, position and possessions" above the love of God. The book delivers a surgical exposition of the emptiness of power and politics without God.

I cannot commend it enough to everyone who would wish to see peace and grace abound in the national capitols of political power instead of selfish ambition and personal glorification."

**—Dr. Ezra Suruma,**
Professor & Chancellor. Office of the President, Kampala,
UGANDA. Minister of Finance, 2005-2009. Visiting fellow at
Brookings, Washington, D.C. 2010-2011


"*Love and Power* offers important insights for leaders who aspire to being 'in the world but not of the world' with real life examples from our nation's capital."

**—Honorable John Moolenaar,**
U.S. House of Representatives, 4th District, Michigan


"When we listen to the words of our nation's political leaders and experience the impact of their decisions, it often appears as though love is in short supply. This is why I am so grateful that Chuck continues to share with us the biblical foundation and compassionate heart that drives his ministry here in DC. *Love and Power* is another such work. Particularly striking to me are Garriott's ministry stories that reveal the kind of love and vulnerability leaders need if they are going to exercise authority in a way that blesses and benefits those they are leading. Read it and find yourself growing as a leader."

—**Rev. Irwyn L. Ince, D. Min.**
Director, GraceDC Institute for Cross-Cultural Mission, Washington D.C. Moderator of the General Assembly, Presbyterian Church in America, 2018-2019

"I found myself rereading chapters as I thought through what it meant for me in public life. In our increasingly self-obsessed society, *Love and Power* is a timely reminder of who we really are, of what Jesus has done for us and how that should impact how we speak and live. This is essential reading not only for those in public life, but for all of us as we seek to die to self and live for Christ."

—**Gordon Lyons,**
Member of the Legislative Assembly, Belfast, Northern Ireland

# LOVE AND POWER

# ALSO BY CHARLES GARRIOTT

*Work Excellence: A Biblical Perspective of Work*

*Obama Prayer: Prayers for the 44th President*

*Rulers: Gospel and Government*

*Prayers for Trump: Petitions for 45th President*

# LOVE AND POWER

## GLIMPSES OF **THE GOSPEL** FOR THOSE ADDICTED TO **SELF**

## CHARLES M. GARRIOTT

RIOTT
*Washington D.C.*

# RIOTT

*Washington D.C.*

Interior design by Jeffrey M. Hall, www.iongdw.com

Cover designed by Christopher Tobias, tobiasdesign.com

ISBN: 978-0-9762004-6-8

RELIGION/SPIRITUAL

Printed in the United States of America

loveandpowerbook.com

First Printing 2019

TO MYSELF....

# CONTENTS

# INTRODUCTION

The air was cold and still. Snow had finished falling and, as the sun began to rise, Washington seemed magical under the fresh white blanket. Alone, I walked the north lawn of the White House to the West Wing, finding my way to the entrance where I waited for my friend. It would be my first experience having breakfast in the Mess.

That single meal has been the extent of my invitation to the executive suite.

I have never met George W. Bush or his late father, Bill Clinton, Barack Obama, Donald Trump, or any others who have held the highest office here in Washington, D.C. I have never corresponded with them, and none would be familiar with my name. Although not personal friends with any of the presidents, I do know something about them. I have spent time with friends, colleagues, and staff members of theirs. I am familiar with the images regularly presented to the world through CNN, FOX, The Washington Post, and The New York Times. I know them, as do you, from their speeches, policies implemented, or, perhaps, through their writings. That is pretty much all the world can know of them. While the media-driven personas and who they truly are may be light years apart, I am not in a position to discern the differences.

In addition to past and current presidents, Washington overflows with myriads who seek positions of significance and influence. Some are elected, as are members of the House and Senate; some are hired to serve them. Many come to make a difference not only within the United States, but also the world. They tend to be bright and focused, with degrees from impressive schools. For a season of their lives they are busy, working in Congress, the White House, federal agencies, think tanks, professional associations, or the media. They all live and work in a unique city, a community defined by power and addiction to self.

For a decade and a half, I have been welcomed in quite a few of these workplaces. Friends from such places have been to our home for dinner discussions or other forums. I have a sense of who these people are, of how they think and live. As a Christian I often have asked myself what impact the gospel has on such a community. Washington regularly is exposed to the gospel, although the gospel is not the dominant influence. What should we expect where Jesus is at work? What difference might he make in the thinking and behavior of those who embrace him? How might he alter such a center of power?

In certain ways, powerful Washingtonians might be compared with a Jew spoken of in the New Testament book of Mark. In the tenth chapter, Mark spotlights the man often referred to as the "rich young ruler" [hereafter, Mr. Ruler]. Like many today he had spiritual concerns. He approached Jesus with a question regarding his qualifications for eternal life. We are not told why the concern was so urgent.

Jesus then asked the Jewish "billionaire" a few basic questions, perhaps similar to those posed in a presidential debate or an MSNBC interview. They were not hard, but rather "softballs." One question pertained to his knowledge of the Old Testament moral law. What citizen of Israel would not know the Ten Commandments? Not only did he know them, but quickly maintained that he had kept them all since childhood. There were no skeletons in this man's closet. He had scored well on the first round, he thought. Confident, he was getting ready for the hard questions. But instead, Jesus made an evaluation and a demand: "Go sell everything you own, give the proceeds to the poor and come and follow Me...." This was not the preacher asking for a tithe. Jesus wanted him to liquidate his entire asset portfolio. And then he wanted his exhausted life. Jesus wants everything—that is the way of the gospel.

Mr. Ruler did not see the fastball coming. I am sure he was surprised. Perhaps there was an awkward silence? We are not told. Mark does inform us of Jesus' view of the man who was addicted to self and his own riches and power. Jesus had compassion on him; but, despite Jesus' love for him, the man walked away sad because he had great wealth. The conversation was over. Or another way of putting it, he was confronted with the idols from which he would not turn. What does that mean? His addiction meant that he was a slave to his possessions, position and reputation. He was addicted to self and all of its glory. He was not ready to liquidate all and follow Jesus. Nothing Jesus said was beyond what the man could afford. Yet, the price seemed, at the time, unreasonable. A most powerful man could not leave the idols of self-love. Although simple and free, the gospel requires you to count the cost. Make no mistake; it is pricey, yet affordable.

So exactly what is this gospel the ruler rejected? The answer is two-fold. One side of the gospel focuses on who we are. Simply put, all of Adam and Eve's children, all mankind, exist in a state of rebellion against a holy God and are in need of reconciliation. We often offend God by what we think, what we say, and the way we behave. This is what the Bible calls sin, rebellion and transgression. The second part of the gospel focuses on the remedy for our dismal position. The only way we can be reconciled to God is through his Son, Jesus Christ. By his perfect life, death on the cross, and resurrection, we are brought into a right relationship with God through accepting his salvation—life—by faith and repentance. What he requires of us is different for each one, as our idols are different, but starts with giving him our lives. Mr. Ruler was not interested in accepting either aspect of the gospel.

This small book has been written to give glimpses of the gospel to Mr. Ruler types and others like him who are self-addicted here in Washington and the rest of the world. When the man was confronted by Christ, he was confronted with his true self. I will not be as succinct as Jesus when talking to the rich young ruler. I do hope, however, that you will have a better appreciation for your need for the gospel regardless of where you live. My prayer is that the gospel will gently confront your own obsessions and sin and show you grace.

# GOSPEL
# DEFINED

# CHAPTER 1

# PRESENCE

///////////////////////////////////////////////////////////////
///////////////////////////////////////////////////////////////

Moving to a new city can be lonely. Arriving in Washington in the Fall of 2003, my wife Debby and I knew virtually no one. After twenty years in the Southwest, in an Oklahoma City pastorate, we had agreed to try life on the East Coast. I sensed a "calling" to Christian ministry among people in government. I visualized spiritually impacting people in the seat of power in one of the most influential cities of the world. Yes, it was naive. Who was I to think it might work? We had no invitation to come and no sure financial support. What future did I presume we had in Washington? I can best describe those first six months as "optimistically depressing."

Other moves in our thirty years of marriage had included instant community. People welcomed us, inviting us to dinner or coffee, and showing us around. We enjoyed parties celebrating our arrival, often accompanied by gifts and tokens of friendship. We were guided to the best grocery stores, doctors, dentists and schools. Occasionally new friends dropped by making sure we were becoming acclimated to the community. None of that happened for us in the Fall of 2003. When we moved to DC, there was no welcoming party, no offers to lend a hand in unpacking the truck. We were on our own and, practically speaking, no one cared that the Garriotts were going to live in the city. To be honest, we had not even thought about the lack of friends and community. We were just glad for the opportunity to take on the adventure.

The Scriptures describe a similar reception for someone who made a significant move over two thousand years ago. Very differently, however, not just anyone was moving. It was Jesus. It was the Son of God who had left not the wide, open skies of Oklahoma City but Heaven to live for a time on earth. The difference is stark. Jesus was the Son of God; I was and remain a relative nobody. So, in some ways it must have been more challenging, right? If you are a nobody, then what do you expect? Did I think there would be an invitation from the White House to drop by for tea? If you were God's eternal Son, you might expect people to be attentive to your presence. But, except within the family, they were not.

## ODD ARRIVAL

Jesus' coming into the world was announced by an angel named Gabriel, who appeared to Mary, a young woman. Gabriel gave details: The coming child was, in fact, the creator of the universe. Even though he was to be born as Mary's infant, he already existed. Indeed, it was a bit confusing. The angel added that the child was to be given the throne of the ancient King David of Israel. Being a king at birth, he would have fit in well in a place like Washington. I should add that the child had a very definite mission. Most of us figure out our purpose and mission well after we are born and, in some cases, well after we have become adults. That was not the case with Jesus. The prophet Isaiah (8th Century BC) said this concerning Jesus:

> For to us a child is born, to us a son is given, and the government will be on his shoulders. And he will be called Wonderful Counselor, Mighty God, Everlasting Father, Prince of Peace. Of the greatness of his government and peace there will be no end.
>
> **Isaiah 9:6,7b**

What a unique calling! The mission of peace Isaiah had spoken of was reiterated by angels who appeared to an assembly of shepherds just after Jesus' birth (Luke 2). Peace was not the only dimension of his charge. When Mary's husband-to-be was not buying her Gabriel story, an angel confronted him in a dream, convincing him that the story was true (Matthew 1). The angel confirmed that Mary was to give birth to a child and his name would be Jesus, since he would save his people from their sin. Giving the world peace would come through the act of saving people from their offensiveness to God. This infant king had a mission of salvation and reconciliation. All this is to say that the world was in great need of true peace. What an understatement! The world was on a totally destructive course.

## ODD **WAYS**

Most of us who believe we have a significant life task do not hesitate to employ every means available to guarantee success. We go after big money, big PR, and, of course, the right people of power and influence to assist us on the mission. Then we need the right clothes, the chauffeur-driven car, and the impressive condo on the right side of the right town. If done correctly, we have the required presence for recognition and success.

Not long ago I was involved in a three-hour evening gathering for heads of state from Africa in downtown Washington, D.C. As a means of accenting the importance of the event, the participants included former President Bill Clinton and the well-known singer, Patti LaBelle. By all standards it was impressive. Held at the Mayflower Hotel and costing, as I was told, around $450,000, the affair had to project the correct image for those attending, right? If you are important and you want the world to know and remember your importance, then all the things mentioned need to be part of your public presence.

Jesus did not seem to know that. He grew up in a rather modest home that never drew anyone's attention. He was not well schooled and did not hang out with the people of influence. And those people of influence, the wealthy and those who really mattered in the Roman Empire, never gave him a nod. (Only King Herod noticed when he heard that the King of the Jews had been born. He then unsuccessfully attempted to take the child's life.) Yes, there were magi from the East who appreciated his coming and made a special visit delivering expensive gifts. But that was about it.

Another noteworthy aspect of Jesus' presence pertains to those with whom he associated. They were twelve nobodies. They were from Galilee.[1] No one of influence came from Galilee: there were no fancy educations, no New York Times best-selling authors and no real Bill-Gates-like wealth. Those moving toward success and making a difference in the world must be seen in the "right company." This is another mistake that Jesus made. The disciples with whom he surrounded himself were, at best, odd.

## ODD TEACHING

Jesus' teaching quickly drew attention in Palestine. Crowds numbering in the thousands spent hours listening to his perspectives on life, heaven and hell. He knew their anxieties and spoke to their felt and unfelt needs. To this day his Sermon on the Mount is quoted and reflected upon by millions. He made it clear that the Old Testament was authoritative as the Word of God and always would be relevant. His teachings were unwavering. He taught with clarity and authority, not only referencing the Old Testament, but also speaking of what would take place both in the near and distant futures. Yes, sometimes the truth presented was more than the crowd could accept; some would leave or threaten to stone him.

Characteristic of his teaching was the way he used questions. Jesus often answered a question with a question of his own, a way of helping those in his makeshift congregation engage with his logic. The account of Mr. Ruler is such an example. At the wealthy man's greeting, "Good Teacher," Jesus responded by asking why the man called him good. The inquisitor did not understand to whom he was speaking. If he had known, he would have followed him. Jesus was not interested in being known as a "Good Teacher." He was interested in people believing that he was Emanuel, "God with us."

# ODD INTENTION

Perhaps what many did not understand nor appreciate was Jesus' persistent direction, his ultimate life purpose, which the angel had spoken about to Joseph in his dream (Matthew 1). He spoke often of how his earthly ministry would end. His teaching at times would provide hints. At other times he was bold and clear. Death was his purpose. Really? That still confuses many. It certainly confused the disciples. When Jesus informed the twelve that he was going to suffer and die, Peter quickly responded by objecting, "This will never happen to you" (Matthew 16). He was mistaken and was rebuked for making such a declaration. Why? Because everything Jesus did on this earth would eventually lead to not just any death, but to a horrific death. It seemed odd then, and perhaps to many now, that his life's purpose was to suffer. How odd.

It is worth noting that prophets who spoke about his coming hundreds of years before his birth foretold of this odd purpose. The Old Testament prophet Isaiah wrote:

He was despised and rejected by mankind, a man of suffering, and familiar with pain. Like one from whom people hide their faces he was despised, and we held him in low esteem. Surely he took up our pain and bore our suffering, yet we considered him punished by God, stricken by him, and afflicted.

**Isaiah 53:3,4**

When he began his ministry, three years before the crucifixion, a man called John the Baptist referred to Jesus as the "Lamb of God," whose purpose was to take away the sin of the world (John

1:29). Without question, that is a huge undertaking. The weight of the world's sin is enormous, and the penalty for offending God to that degree is even greater. To fulfill such a purpose meant that Jesus would need to suffer far beyond what anyone could imagine.

The world to this day continues to write and speak about the presence of Jesus. For much of the world, however, his coming and life make no sense; it will remain confusing unless and until you discover your need for him.

While many people today are interested in the teachings, moral life and kind acts of Jesus, they may have no interest in following him or surrendering to him as Lord. That was the case with Mr. Ruler. He sought after Jesus, was interested in his teaching, but had no interest in following him. He would not give up his idols for anyone. Perhaps it just seemed too strange. Yet, Jesus alone can make a difference in the lives of those addicted to self.

# CHAPTER 2

# OFFENSE

I t was June 2006 when I attended my first White House staff function in the Treaty Room of the Old Executive Building. Scanning the crowd of some 100 people, I knew no one except my friend, the honored guest for the event. Seeing him deep in conversation as he greeted his company, I waited. I began to make small talk with a few of the guests. Some worked in White House Legislative Affairs, some were speechwriters for the president, and others had moved into the lobbying side of Washington. As usual, I avoided disclosing the nature of my work as long as possible; divulging my vocation tends to kill the flow of conversation. "Oh, you're in ministry?" Either they don't value my work, or they feel the need to move on to a safer part of the room. As I continued noting the room dynamics, it was evident that most guests knew others and engaged in conversations. They were comfortable with each other. Those attending were attractive, well educated, and ambitious. They worked for the President of the United States. Most came from other parts of the country to be change agents. They wanted to make a difference.

These are common events inside the beltway. People are always coming and going. It's one reception, inaugural ball, or dinner party after the next. As I meet and think about these beltway insiders, I ask myself, who are these people really? What do they actually believe? I am not asking about their political affiliations, career paths, or level of importance. I am asking how do they see themselves. How do they see God? They all look civil, clean and neat. Acceptable. What would it look like to see these acquaintances from the perspective of the Scriptures—through the eyes of God?

## IS THERE **A PROBLEM?**

In the middle of the New Testament book of Mark, we read about a gathering near the capital city, Jerusalem. Pharisees and teachers of the law, leaders in the Jewish religious community, complained to Jesus that some of his disciples had not properly cleaned their hands according to tradition. (When returning from the marketplace one would "ceremonially wash." This would make you "clean" after coming into contact with those in the community who were unacceptable.) The leaders were offended. Jesus used the opportunity to address big questions. Who were these people really? What was the true condition of their hearts? Jesus responded:

"Listen to me, everyone, and understand this. Nothing outside a man can make him 'unclean' by going into him." He went on: "What comes out of a man is what makes him 'unclean.' For from within, out of men's hearts, come evil thoughts, sexual immorality, theft, murder, adultery, greed, malice, deceit, lewdness, envy, slander, arrogance and folly. All these evils come from inside and make a man 'unclean.'"

Mark 7:14-16;21,22

# THE STENCH OF
# SELF-RIGHTEOUSNESS

In a sense, Jesus agreed with the Scribes and Pharisees. They found the disciples unacceptable, and so did he. The difference was why.

Let's face it: we enjoy placing ourselves above others, pronouncing judgment. It feels great to be superior. It's addictive. Places like Washington, D.C., and the general political environment, thrive on being superior. A common pastime is to ask: "Who can we pass judgment on today?" "Who can we destroy for political gain?" We thereby develop our own self-righteousness. I understand this; I too participate in this evil sport.

The Jewish establishment of Jesus' day lived by a system of traditions that although appearing to be supportive of Scriptures were not. Ceremonial washing was a means of placing judgment on others. If a Jew had been around Gentiles, or others who were considered unclean, at the marketplace, he was required to wash by sprinkling water on his hands in the manner prescribed to make him ceremonially clean. The Pharisees and teachers of the Law were offended that Jesus' disciples did not observe this tradition and pronounced them unacceptable. Yet, the Jewish leaders were the ones Jesus found to be offensive. Jesus' words in response to them were very direct and forceful: "...you nullify the word of God by your tradition that you have handed down" (v. 13). The truth is that none of us escapes his words: We all stand condemned.

My lack of cleanliness makes me unacceptable to God.[2] What I eat or do outwardly, however, is not the problem. To understand what makes me unclean, unacceptable to God, I need to see what is inside by observing what is revealed in my life: my thoughts, words, and actions. This informs me of the truth about those at the White House staff event and about Chuck Garriott.

As a boy growing up in the family of a plumber, I found myself installing and unclogging sewer pipes. Sometimes my Saturday morning job was to pump out the septic tank of our home. This was never pleasant. Everything put down the sink or flushed down the toilet was in there. Jesus helps us to look at the sewage in each of our lives, what the Bible calls the heart, or the inner man. He does not leave it up to our imaginations to figure out what makes up our septic tank heart. "What comes out of a man is what makes him 'unclean.' For from within, out of men's hearts, come evil thoughts..." (vv. 20,21).

## COMMUNITY **INSULTED**

Jesus' description of the unclean condition of the heart shows what is true selfishness: depriving others of the benefits that belong to them. What do theft, murder, adultery, and greed have in common? They take place out of passion for, or idolatry of, self:

selfish ambition, selfish gain, self-promotion. When tempted to take something that belongs to another, one is consumed with the pursuit of a cheap form of happiness—obtained at the expense of another. This "me" idol takes another's property (theft), another's life (murder), or another's spouse (adultery). Sometimes it is pure greed. At other times a relationship that has grown ugly reveals the depth of our wayward self— not a pretty picture.

But the ugliness surfaces in other ways. Jesus' perspective on the heart includes additional dimensions of selfishness. We believe that the only way to survive within a community is deception. We want our community to think that we are something that we are not. The deceptive mask is a way of sending a message that the world should see us as attractive. Again, the "me" idol feeds on self-centeredness at the expense of the truth. Arrogance, and all its accompanying traits, is a common force among those pursuing or wielding power in this city.

Jesus' view of the life and heart challenged the statements made by Mr. Ruler. Yes, he was interested in Jesus and had a true respect for his teaching. But, if I understand him correctly, there was a discrepancy: Jesus saw a problem; the seeker did not. I am sure that I too see myself as being better than I am. But in either case, that is hugely problematic.

# IS THERE A REMEDY?

If it is true that our hearts are swollen with selfish desires, we will not be able to purge ourselves of such desires and habits on our own. The person who sees his or her heart for what it is, and for the offense that it causes God and neighbor will feel the need for cleansing. So, what do we do?

The Jews tried to deal with their selfishness by instituting a system. This system focused not upon the heart, but upon being outwardly clean. This is what Jesus refers to as "traditions." In doing so, the Jews belittled sin and its offensive impact. They reduced sin to something that they could address in their own strength. Their self-remedies failed. Jesus saw this as nothing more than hypocrisy, deception, and vain worship, trading the truth for a lie, and living out life based upon the lie. These leaders seemed to believe that they could do what only God can do. There are many ways that we deal with sin. If we are honest, we are not much different than the Jews of Jesus' day.

So, what is the right response? Should I despair and be hopeless? Is there anything I can change? Nothing. And yet, I can seek another who promises true redemption, rest and relief.

Mr. Rulers in a place like Washington will only pursue Jesus when the burden of self is overwhelming. There is no system or formula that can remedy our hopeless condition. There is one Savior. No one comes to Jesus without seeing his own need. Jesus is not in the entertainment business. He is in the business of redeeming people from their self-deception. If we do not see ourselves as Jesus sees us, then we will never seek him. That is a tough perspective for those in the business of government and power.

CHAPTER 3

# THE COST

I t was a cold Christmas in Oklahoma City in the mid-1980s. Some of our acquaintances had fallen on hard times in a state punished by the Penn Square Bank collapse. My family, friends and I had planned to spend the day together, opening gifts and eating holiday foods while enjoying the warmth of the fire. But I was on my way to Children's Hospital. The family I was visiting did not need work or holiday greetings: they needed a miracle.

My memory of that sad December day has never faded. The seven-month-old little girl lay in an oxygen tent that became her last home after unsuccessful surgery on a brain tumor. When I arrived, her mother and father sat quietly next to their infant's bed. Other family members were present, comforting each other as the child's breathing slowly vanished. It was not more than a few hours after I arrived when she took her last breath and slipped into eternity. Along with the others, all I could do was weep as the lifeless body was removed from the bed and placed in the arms of her mother. This was Christmas? It was a true picture of the "sting of death."

Throughout my years in ministry I have spent time with people facing imminent death. These are never easy times for the dying or for the family and friends caring for them. What must it have been like to sit close to the Son of God only hours before he was to take the path to the place of his last breath?

The Gospel of Matthew provides a disturbing picture of what Jesus went through before facing the cross. He went with his disciples to Gethsemane where he instructed them to watch while he went aside to pray. His three-year ministry with them was coming to an end. Their short time in Jerusalem had been confusing at best. They did not understand many of the things he had told them. This was especially so regarding what he had said about his own suffering and death. Now for that dreadful evening we are given some details:

> He took Peter and the two sons of Zebedee along with him, and he began to be sorrowful and troubled. Then he said to them, "My soul is overwhelmed with sorrow to the point of death. Stay here and keep watch with me." Going a little farther, he fell with his face to the ground and prayed, "My Father, if it is possible, may this cup be taken from me. Yet not as I will, but as you will." Then he returned to his disciples and found them sleeping. "Could you men not keep watch

with me for one hour?" he asked Peter. 'Watch and pray so that you will not fall into temptation. The spirit is willing, but the body is weak."

**Matthew 26:37-41**

# FAITHFUL FRIENDS?

Leaving Peter, James, and John a mere stone's throw away, Jesus fell with his face to the ground and prayed. During this time of appeal to the Father, a number of things took place. His agony was so great that Luke records that his "sweat was like drops of blood falling to the ground" (Luke 22:44). At the same time an angel appeared and strengthened him. The weight of what was about to happen placed an enormous strain on the Savior. And what were the disciples doing? Sleeping. How could they be so callous? Even after Jesus had wakened them multiple times, they fell back asleep again. The disciples seemed totally insensitive.

We might think that if we had been there, it would have been different. We would have stood nearby and been alert to what was happening. We would have tried to understand his pain. We would have offered to serve him. We would have gathered with the others and prayed for him. Perhaps.

In all likelihood, I would have behaved like the disciples. It is an amazingly sad picture that they were too exhausted to appreciate being present for the most significant event in all of history. They lacked the ability to be other-oriented. They seemed to lack the insight to ask important questions. What was actually taking place? What did Jesus' prayer represent? Why was this so significant an occasion?

## THE CUP

On first reading Scripture's description, one might think that Jesus' soul was overwhelmed with the realities of his imminent death, Peter's denial, the trial, the lashings, and the pain of the cross. But this was not the case. "My soul," he said, "is overwhelmed to the point of death" (Matthew 26:38). What would cause him to experience this degree of pain, sorrow, and trouble? The source of his sorrow and agony was the "cup" that he had to drink.

Interestingly, many read this passage without fully feeling its impact. We have heard and read accounts of those who have experienced horrific things—the details of someone being mauled to death by a bear or eaten by a shark or stabbed by an attacker. These are not pleasant to read. Yet, we find little discomfort in reading the Gethsemane account. Why? We have little understanding of the meaning of the "cup." The Scriptures teach that the "cup" of which Jesus spoke was the wrath of God.[3]

No one's rage comes close to the anger of God. Many Christians ignore this truth. Few regularly praise God for his anger. I know of few hymns or songs that help those in the church sing of God's wrath. We may disregard his fury; but Jesus could not.

## ANTIQUITY

We first read about the anger of God in the Old Testament. God-sized fury cannot be overlooked. Examining the details of the flood in Genesis, we are confronted with the offenses of wicked men and God's holy justice. Later in the Old Testament we read specifically about the "cup."

Awake, awake! Rise up, O Jerusalem, you who have drunk from the hand of the Lord the cup of his wrath, you who have drained to its dregs the goblet that makes men stagger.

**Isaiah 51:17**

The "chalice" of which Jesus was speaking in the garden was the cup of wrath mentioned in Isaiah. Wrath means deep, intense anger and indignation.[4] Some have noticed that the Scriptures refer to God's anger, fury, and wrath more than his love and tenderness. Nahum also speaks of his wrath:

The LORD is a jealous and avenging God; the LORD takes vengeance and is filled with wrath. The LORD takes vengeance on his foes and maintains his wrath against his enemies.

**Nahum1:2**

In contrast, God's anger differs from ours. Anger, to us, often is the irrational, uncontrolled outburst that comes out of wounded pride or plain bad temper. We become frustrated because things have not gone the way we wanted. As a result, we verbally or physically lash out at someone. Do you? God's wrath is his righteous reaction to our sin—it is his justice at work. The Apostle Paul refers to it in Romans:

The wrath of God is being revealed from heaven against all the godlessness and wickedness of men who suppress the truth by their wickedness.

**Romans 1:18**

In the garden Jesus understood that in going to the cross, he would be drinking God's wrath. Perhaps Matthew draws our attention to this moment in the garden because we see there the wrath and grace of God come together. Jesus did drink the cup. He drank the cup of God's wrath that you and I should have consumed. It is the ultimate expression of his love for us. That act of love requires a response.

# RESPONSE

The writer of the book of Hebrews reminds us of the amazing frame of mind Jesus had in taking upon himself the anger of God "...for the joy that was set before him" (Hebrews 12:2). This was the nature of Christ's selflessness. In light of this, we are told to "fix our eyes on Jesus, the author and perfecter of our faith" (v.2).

The more we understand what Jesus experienced on our behalf, the better we begin to grasp the depths of his love and grace. Jesus died for those he loved, those who own their sinful condition, and believe that they justly deserve the Father's wrath. The offensiveness that Jesus spoke about in Mark 7, what comes from the heart (our lust, hate, greed, slander, arrogance, pride, discontentment, idolatry), is what caused Jesus such pain. We offend God when we attempt to replace him with possessions, positions, and prestige. Those never fully satisfy and never replace the need for God. It just does not work.

The rich young rulers of the world (including those in government, business, finance, education, and media) usually do not see it. They view themselves as being better than they are. They see their ways as being superior to God's ways. They rule themselves. The picture of the great suffering that God-in-the-flesh experienced is confusing.

Are we any different? The gospel means nothing until we see the need for Jesus' suffering and are horrified that we caused it. Jesus stood in our place in a way that no one else who has ever lived could have. Those who accept the truth of what he did understand what it means to humbly seek him—with thanksgiving and appreciation for what he did in taking upon himself the Father's anger.

Modeling such humility and selflessness might make a difference in places like Washington and other world power centers.

CHAPTER 4

# HUMILITY

When I was a child, a man called Old Ben lived near our home in Granite, Maryland. Ben did odd jobs as a laborer when not working on the back of a garbage truck. Occasionally he would be found lying drunk near the road, foaming at the mouth. Our neighbor Mr. Ford, with my father's help, would drive him to his dilapidated home back in the field and put him in bed. He had very little, but he was part of our rural community.

An hour's drive south, in Washington, not far from where I now live in Adams-Morgan, I see similar persons.[5] The difference is that Old Ben had a home. Many of those on the street here do not. Neither Ben nor those on the sidewalks near my home would be considered an acceptable model for raising children. You would never hear a loving parent say to a child, "I hope someday you become poor like Old Ben." There is nothing attractive about poverty. Here in Washington countless policies have been debated and instituted to fight the endless war on the depressing social condition. Poverty is not something we desire or are drawn toward; but, this is not necessarily so with God.

## IMAGES OF REDEMPTION

Luke gives many redemptive pictures, images of salvation. First, Jewish parents understood that according to God's covenant with Abraham, a male child, on the eighth day after his birth, was to be circumcised (Genesis 17). Circumcision was a sign that represented union with God. God established an everlasting covenant between himself, Abraham, and Abraham's descendants. For all generations to come, God unilaterally would be committed to them. Second, the one to be circumcised was Jesus, whose name in the Greek means salvation, rescue, deliverance (Matthew 1:21). Third, in Exodus 13, God instructs his people, the Israelites, about consecrating the firstborn child or firstborn of their flock. The instruction came as God was delivering his people from Egypt. When following this aspect of the law, the Jewish parent remembered the time of slavery in Egypt and the freedom given Israel by God. This foreshadowed the salvation to come in Jesus.

## POVERTY

Following the birth of Jesus, the apostle Luke spotlighted the Jewish custom of male children being circumcised, the occasion of purification and consecration.

On the eighth day, when it was time to circumcise him, he was named Jesus, the name the angel had given him before he had been conceived. When the time of their purification according to the Law of Moses had been completed, Joseph and Mary took him to Jerusalem to present him to the Lord (as it is written in the Law of the Lord, "Every firstborn male is to be consecrated to the Lord"), and to offer a sacrifice in keeping with what is said in the Law of the Lord: "a pair of doves or two young pigeons."

**Luke 2: 21-24**

Joseph and Mary offered a sacrifice to the Lord when consecrating the baby Jesus. What governed this offering? In the Old Testament book of Leviticus, God informed the Israelites that a pregnant woman who gave birth remained ceremonially unclean for seven days. On the eighth day, the male child was to be circumcised. After a prescribed period of time, the family would present a year-old lamb for a burnt offering and a young pigeon for a sin offering. Once the offering had been made, the mother was clean. The Law, however, gave consideration to the economically disadvantaged. The poor who could not offer a lamb were to offer two doves or two pigeons.

We assume that Joseph and Mary had financial means to travel from Galilee, look for lodging, and take care of themselves for a time. It was limited, however, and when the time came for her purification according to the Law of Moses, they offered two birds. They had humble means. I find it amazing that these two people, given the responsibility of caring for the Redeemer, God-made-flesh, were poor. That is absurd! We would have made sure that every possible resource was provided for the God-child. We tend to think of poverty as a sign of someone unblessed by God. Clearly, Jesus presents a different picture of poverty.

## DEPTH OF **POVERTY**

A parent does not want a beloved child to grow up and become poor; in fact, much of a child's training is dedicated to learning how to be productive so that there will be no threat of poverty. Although hard to grasp, Luke reminds us that God called his Son to a life of poverty. God coming in the flesh was the greatest act of humility in all of history. The apostle Paul, in 2 Corinthians, says:

> For you know the grace of our Lord Jesus Christ, that though he was rich, yet for your sakes he became poor, so that you through his poverty might become rich.
>
> **2 Corinthians 8:9**

The Prophet Isaiah tells us of the greatness of God (Isaiah 40). He refers to his power as displayed in creation. In addition, he draws a comparison with the nations of the world and speaks of them as nothing but drops in a bucket relative to God. Further, Isaiah describes the intellectual ability and other attributes of God that cannot be understood at all by mortals. In every way he is far beyond our ability to fathom. And yet, the Son of God is described in Isaiah 53:

He was despised and rejected by men, a man of sorrows, and familiar with suffering. Like one from whom men hide their faces he was despised, and we esteemed him not. Surely he took up our infirmities and carried our sorrows, yet we considered him stricken by God, smitten by him, and afflicted. But he was pierced for our transgressions, he was crushed for our iniquities; the punishment that brought us peace was upon him, and by his wounds we are healed.

(vv. 3-5)

How could it be that the one who created the universe and the world in which we live, and who keeps it running in an orderly manner by his providence and power, willingly experienced such suffering and humiliation? Did Jesus' humiliation come only when his life was ending? On the contrary, Jesus suffered his entire life. Born in a place fit only for animals, he was forced, with his parents, to run and hide in Egypt. He grew up in poverty. We see Jesus' humiliation when he entered the wilderness for forty days and nights. He was insulted by Satan and received constant verbal abuse from the religious leaders and others in the Jewish community. Even the unbelief of his own disciples must have been humbling. He willingly endured all of it.

Toward the end of his ministry, his humiliation intensified in his taking the cup of God's wrath, as mentioned before. He was handed over by one of his own disciples, resulting in arrest, trial before Pilot, flogging, and hateful screams for his crucifixion. Still, the humiliation was not over: Forced to make the painful walk to Golgotha and then hanging on a cross was perhaps the height of his humiliation, but not the end. He spoke a number of times while on the cross and then breathed his last.

## GIFT OF **POVERTY**

To experience death is to admit that one has offended God and is, therefore, experiencing the penalty. Death is judicial in nature. Romans says "the wages of sin is death" (6:23). The Scriptures are clear that when Adam and Eve sinned, God said that the result of disobedience would be death. God withdrew himself from their presence. God withdrew his blessings and poured out his wrath. That is what Jesus spoke of when praying about the cup (Ezekiel 23:32-34). Jesus' ultimate humiliation was to take upon himself God's anger that belonged to us.

It is one thing for a person of wealth to give a portion of his or her income to a worthy cause or for another's need. It is another matter for that person to give sacrificially in a manner that causes the sacrifice even of one's own life. This is the gospel, the magnificent news. Jesus became poor so that others would become rich.

Herein lies the challenge for Mr. Ruler and those like him. Those who embrace the gospel soon learn that a spirit of poverty is expected from all who want to follow Jesus. Mr. Ruler was not overjoyed with the prospect of living the rest of his life without wealth, position, and glory. When Jesus gave him the instruction to rid himself of the distraction of wealth, he left and went away in sadness. He was not able to see the riches and nature of the true wealth that was waiting for him in Jesus.

This is the challenge facing Washington as well. Yes, our leaders must address aggressively the problem of poverty and its devastating consequences. At the same time, our wealthy leaders need true poverty of spirit to change the way others are viewed and treated. What a different world it would be if Christ-like poverty and humility were the norm in the capital of the richest nation of the world!

CHAPTER 5

# POWER

Several years ago, a diplomat serving in an embassy on Massa-
chusetts Avenue told me he believed the District of Columbia was the most powerful city of the world. Interestingly, he
did not view Washington as a place of service, but of supremacy.
Beijing, London, New Delhi, Tokyo, all of which I have visited
numerous times, are fascinating and influential world cities. Their
people, foods, cultures, and histories could take a lifetime to com-
prehend. Such government centers not only affect their own people, but also influence nations around the globe. Washington and
other capitals alter economies, business trends, employment, and
the use of defense systems. Washington decision-makers direct
policies monitored by almost every nation. The sense of hope

and peace can be extended or shattered by our nation's leadership within a manner of minutes. It is a place of power.

In his letter to the church in Rome in the first century, the Apostle Paul wrote of a different form of power:

> I am not ashamed of the gospel, because it is the power of God for the salvation of everyone who believes..."
>
> **Romans 1:16**

## KNOWING **GOD?**

Jesus, speaking to religious leaders about their misunderstanding of the Scriptures, painted them as ignorant of the power of God. Perhaps he would say the same of us today? What exactly does "the power of God" mean? And why should it interest us?

The word power in Romans comes from the Greek "dynamis," ancestor of the English word dynamite. The term evokes images of powerful forces such as the sun or a nuclear bomb, or, perhaps of personal autonomy or political authority. Power is a big deal in Washington and other capitals. And it was a big deal to Mr. Ruler. It should not surprise us that Paul frequently mentions this attribute of God. Both Old and New Testaments frequently highlight God's power. Isaiah describes God thus:

> See, the Sovereign LORD comes with power, and his arm rules for him...

Who has measured the waters in the hollow of his
hand, or with the breadth of his hand marked off
the heavens?

**Isaiah 40:10,12**

Creation reflects God's nature. Isaiah challenges those interested in understanding God to contemplate the world's massive
bodies of water which cover 70% of its surface. The average ocean's
depth is over two miles. Near the U.S. territorial Island of Guam,
the Pacific floor lies nearly thirty-six thousand feet deep.[6]

Isaiah points us upward to the heavens. Since we can see only
a small portion, apprehending the vastness is nearly impossible.
If you could fly at the speed of light (186,000 miles per second),
travel from one side of our solar system to the other would take
over five hours. Yet, our solar system within the Milky Way gal-
axy compares proportionately with the difference between a smart
phone and the continent of Europe. We are told that the universe
is well over a hundred thousand times the size of the Milky Way.[7]
The size and complexity of the great oceans and, indeed, the universe, demonstrate the greatness and majesty of God.

How did God create all this? He did not use his hands. He
simply spoke. He created out of nothing, by the mere power of his
word. Think about that. More than impressive, that is true power!

## POWER AND **REDEMPTION**

Paul argues that the same divine attribute shown in God's work
of creation also applied to his work of redemption. Paul could have
accented God's grace, mercy or love when discussing the gospel in
Romans 1. Instead he focused on God's power. Why? Because our

offense against him is so enormous. It took an omnipotent God who spoke the universe into being to address our sin.

We have a puny view of our offense toward God. We see our sin as an irritating fly at a picnic. We can fairly easily use a fly swatter to kill a fly. If I suggested to you that I preferred to use a shotgun, you might think that was a "bit much." Use of the shotgun, however, would lead you to think that I believed the destruction of a fly needed the additional power of a gun. You would better understand my view of how to resolve the problem of the uninvited fly, even if you thought it overkill. The demonstration of God's power through the gospel is some indication of the extent of our offense to God. Mr. Ruler's disobedience—and Chuck Garriott's—is far more offensive than he or I could ever know on this side of heaven. It took more than a small act of God for it to be resolved.

I like to view myself as the kindly old grandfather type, reading a book to my grandchildren, having just served them a glass of milk with their cookies. In contrast, God sees me and my life as the Timothy McVeigh who just exploded a 4,800-pound bomb that took the lives of many innocent people, including grandparents and children. It is no small matter to seek and obtain forgiveness under such circumstances. In order for God to satisfy his justice, to extend his holy forgiveness, he had to apply his power through the gospel.

Mr. Ruler viewed himself as very powerful. His power had enabled him to build a kingdom, to establish his influence. He saw himself as a person with the ability to get things done. This is why the world knew of him and perhaps envied what he had. How fine it would be to have a piece of it all!

Jesus presented an entirely different kind of power. His redemptive work was the only way our offense could be addressed. He did not need a monumental display of power. The gospel message is the declaration that all who have ever lived are in great trouble because of their offense to the holy God. The good news of the gospel is that the God-Man, Jesus Christ, lived a perfect life, died a horrific death on the cross, was buried in a tomb, and, three days later, rose from the grave, conquering death. He lives today as King of kings and the Lord of lords. We either submit to him or remain in a state of obnoxious rebellion.

Washington is an enormous power plant. It often thrives on the egos of those who see themselves as the world's power brokers. They come on a mission, with agendas, to make a better world (or perhaps to make a world according to their own personal values). It is all about influence and power. It is intoxicating. So, Jesus' life of poverty is not often a welcomed model. It can be confusing. The challenge for Mr. Ruler and those like him here in Washington is to acknowledge that there is one true King who, alone, truly holds all power. The gospel is a picture of his sovereign power that is wrapped in grace and love and transforms those who receive it. The power of God as demonstrated by the gospel will not be a secret. It will be evident in a number of ways.

First, God's power in individual lives will be demonstrated by their faith. Belief in what we cannot see is noteworthy. Faith, in fact, is so absurd that the world, according to the Apostle Paul, will claim that we are fools.

> Jews demand miraculous signs and Greeks look for wisdom, but we preach Christ crucified: a stumbling block to Jews and foolishness to Gentiles, but to those whom God has called, both Jews and Greeks, Christ the power of God and the wisdom of God.
>
> **1 Corinthians 1:22-24**

The presence of faith causes an awareness of sin and a desire to repent, to turn from the sin. The person who has saving faith will find that he or she is no longer comfortable with the old ways of thinking and living.

Second, he or she will pursue the object of faith with worship, prayer and instruction. Those whose lives are transformed by the power of the gospel spend time with the Lord in corporate and private worship. This includes reading and studying the Old and New Testaments. Jesus was clear about the need to pursue the Scriptures when speaking to his disciples as recorded in the gospel of John (15:7).

Third, this absurd foolish faith will be evident in the way a person lives out his or her life in relationship to others. In the Epistle of Galatians, the Apostle Paul speaks about the fruit of the Spirit, which begins with love (Galatians 5). Although thinking about others in a way that promotes their best interest is not easy, this faith demands that we pursue them with Christ's love, looking for ways of serving and caring, putting our own interests last. How needed here in Washington! Over time I have seen such gospel power transform individuals and their communities.

In one case I witnessed a Christ-following couple sacrificially serve a single mom by taking care of her infant children on the weekends. It was a way of giving the mother a needed break to improve her health. The couple had moved to Washington after finishing graduate school. They both had demanding jobs. For a number of years one of them had a job at the White House that would not allow him to return home before ten o'clock at night. In addition, he traveled to Asia monthly in support of the president's bilateral and multilateral meetings. The young couple often finished a long work week exhausted; yet, they wanted to see this small family do better, even though it meant limiting their time to catch up on the weekends. Their acts of service made a big difference in the lives of this mother and her young children. More importantly, the caring relationship had a significant impact in the lives of those at the church, showing the congregation what a loving family in a tough circumstance looks like and providing a testimony of how God is moving in all walks of life in this "powerful" city. Such a show of love is a picture of what the power of the gospel will do.

In order for us to fully appreciate the gospel, we need to see how it demonstrates God's omnipotence. The impact of that powerful gospel will not be kept secret but will be evident to a city and world that is starving for its presence.

# PRESENCE

Man's maker was made man,
that He, Ruler of the stars, might nurse at His
mother's breast;
that the Bread might hunger,
the Fountain thirst,
the Light sleep,
the Way be tired on its journey;
that the Truth might be accused of false witness,
the Teacher be beaten with whips,
the Foundation be suspended on wood;
that Strength might grow weak;
that the Healer might be wounded;
that Life might die.

– Augustine of Hippo (Sermons 191.1)

# GOSPEL
# APPLIED

# CHAPTER 6

# DEATH

I reached my 60/40 window in 2014; that is, I celebrated my 60th birthday and my 40th wedding anniversary with Debby in the same year. One tends to be a bit reflective at this stage—at least regarding what one can remember. In reconsidering my life, I've been asking questions: What have I accomplished? What would I do differently? What have I learned? Thinking back on past years, I am reminded of the benefits of marriage, especially when dealing with the "monster of self." My wife Debby has been more than kind and patient with me over the years. A robust measure of my self-centeredness surfaces when we discuss our home here in Adams-Morgan. Having been in a ten-year renovation marathon, we often have diverged in views on what we will change. Guess who wins.

My relationship with Jesus exposes a deeper dimension of self-centeredness. In the Gospel of Matthew, Jesus had a dialogue with the disciples regarding his identity. Peter accurately acknowledged that Jesus was the Christ, God's anointed one. Many tensions followed. Jesus instructed his disciples that he had to go to Jerusalem and suffer at the hands of the Jewish leaders. The turmoil would end in his death. Yet on the third day he would be resurrected. In response to Jesus' prediction, Peter rebuked him: "Never, Lord! This shall never happen to you!" (Matthew 16:22). What took place next had to sting. Jesus turned to Peter and said: "Get behind me, Satan! You are a stumbling block to me; you do not have in mind the things of God, but the things of men" (v. 23). Then without a pause, Jesus addressed all those present.:

> If anyone would come after me, he must deny himself and take up his cross and follow me. For whoever wants to save his life will lose it, but whoever loses his life for me will find it. What good will it be for a man if he gains the whole world, yet forfeits his soul? Or what can a man give in exchange for his soul?
>
> **Matthew 16:24-26**

Many of us can remember having fallen out of favor with a teacher or professor and found ourselves in a tense spot in the classroom. Perhaps Peter too felt this, both the sting of Jesus' rebuke, as well as a bit of confusion. He appeared to be protective of the Master. Would the other disciples have thought Peter correct in wanting to see Jesus sheltered from the suffering and death of which he spoke? They had misunderstood the significance of what was to come, as well as what it meant to think and live in communion with Jesus.

Matthew underscores not only the need for Jesus to die, but, in a manner of speaking, for those who follow him also to experience death. In fact, it would be reasonable to say that anyone contemplating the gospel needs to have a serious conversation regarding the place of "death to self," that is, following Jesus' lead, rather than our own preferences, in all areas of life. This kind of death is foreign to the narcissistic personalities prevalent today. Narcissism and the gospel do not mix. This is not good news for Mr. Ruler types. Nor is it pleasant news for me. As a means of better understanding Jesus' death and the call to die to self, consider the following questions.

## MY PERSPECTIVE **OFFENDS** THE **GOSPEL?**

Jesus often informed the disciples of what was to take place. As Isaiah 53 had warned, the servant who would bear our sin would suffer. This suffering is the focus of God's redemptive plan as proclaimed in Genesis 3 and expounded upon in the New Testament letters (Hebrews 9, for example). It was hard for the disciples to grasp this truth. Suffering and bloodshed are not easy to accept. It was, however, critically important for Jesus to go through the coming horror. Peter was not in sync with the timing and particulars of this crucial season of God's redemptive work.

Peter and his views should be considered. He was spiritually-minded and ministry-oriented. The man had left everything to follow Jesus. He gave up his fishing career and old life to do what few would be willing to do. Yet, when reminded of the most significant event in God's redemptive plan, he became an obstructionist. He was not cheering Jesus along in his work. He was in the way. He had no reason to withhold his rebuke. Why? I am not sure I know. It seems that Peter had developed an agenda that he believed superseded Jesus' agenda. After all, not only had Peter given up a great deal, he also had "bought into" the work and ministry of Jesus. Naturally he and the others would think of ways to increase the significant success demonstrated by large crowds, people being healed, fed, and taught. Why do anything that would distract from success? Jesus' declared direction seemed to Peter to ignore all the great things that were taking place. But Jesus was not the problem. Peter simply failed to think and direct his life in a way that would support God's redeeming plan. Somehow God's strategy to save those who offended him was not important to Peter.

God's purposes will not be altered by our inability to appreciate his ways. The issue for Peter was not his ability to alter one stage of God's set purpose. The question for this disciple was whether he would think and act in harmony with God.

If Mr. Ruler were present, I am certain he would have expressed an opinion much like Peter's. Perhaps he would have fit in well with the twelve? How do we think and live in ways that demonstrate in part or in whole those qualities we see in Peter? In what ways are we like Mr. Ruler? Too often we fail to appreciate what it means to follow the sovereign will of our gracious Lord when it comes to our inner heart, family, relationships, work, finances, church, future, or present disappointments. Death to our particular perspectives and ways is what will take place when we are being transformed by Jesus.

# A MEMORIAL VIEW **OF JESUS?**

When I think of Jesus, do I think principally of what he did in history, in my past personal life, or of what he is doing at present? Peter and the others had left much to follow Jesus. Mark 10 speaks of this fact. I am sure that it was a great challenge for them to leave all that was comfortable and familiar to them and follow Jesus. Yet, in time, they were able to see what an incredible honor it was to be in such a position as apostles. Life had become rather dynamic. Think of what it must have been like to witness the calming of the storm, the healing and feeding of thousands, the paralytic who was lowered down from the roof and walked out of the house healed, Lazarus' resurrection from the dead. These were miracles!

The past is important. Yet, God is not only interested in the past. He is the God of the past, present, and future. He is working in our world today just as much as he was in the past. The disciples needed to keep up and stay connected to the present Jesus. Their lives became somewhat comfortable as their work grew and expanded. Jesus' words threatened the new position of ease. I have the same sin. I want to study and enjoy the historical Jesus that the Scriptures speak about. It is safe. I want to look back and enjoy what Jesus has done in my life.

But we cannot afford to practice a memorial view of him as if only the past is relevant. To die to self means I am ready now for whatever change or challenge he has for me. It does not work to rest on an outdated past.

# LOOKING FOR **LIFE?**

Things were going to change for Peter and the disciples. It would be hard. It would test the source of life for them. Jesus saw their obsession with the preservation of self for life. Their satisfaction was in their existence, not their Lord. It is possible that the world may applaud your success and world-class accomplishments. Yet those who embrace the gospel value the loss of self, life, and all that goes with it. "For whoever wants to save his life will lose it, but whoever loses his life for me will find it" (Matthew 16:25).

These were not business investors who were self-centered and cared nothing for others. These men were engaged in strategic spiritual work. But their work of ministry as experienced in the past had become what gave them meaning. And this was true for Peter. I must regularly ask the question, "What idols have settled in my life? What do I really seek to make me happy?

The move to Washington, D.C., had been a most humiliating and difficult change for me. Leaving comfortable Oklahoma City was hard for our family. Debby gave up her home, church, life and friends. We would be separated from most of our children. Even after five years I did not feel settled. I found that I greatly missed the previous twenty years of pastoring our congregation. Preaching and teaching had been an enormous privilege. I would not have a pulpit. Somehow, I took what was good and acceptable and made it into what would give me life and purpose. My idol was my past life, and I greatly missed it. I think that is what happened to Peter. He somehow no longer needed Jesus. He needed his vision of what Jesus needed to be. If my joy and satisfaction are gone, I need to see if I too have made something else my savior.

## DEFINING **DEATH?**

What does it mean to carry a cross? Those seen carrying their cross in the streets of any Roman city had been sentenced to death. The cross was the sign that the person had been found guilty of a serious crime and must now die. It was not a sign of glory, but humiliation. Peter needed to hear Jesus' words, "If anyone would come after me, he must deny himself and take up his cross and follow me" (v. 24). He needed to give up his views, his perspective of his life and his ministry, and surrender to what the King of the universe was about to do. Instead of rebuking God, he needed to seek the means of serving the purposes of God. How well do I accept the exhortation to die to self? What part of my life must I give up now? Is it possible that my agenda is foreign to God? Am I dying to self when it comes to my marriage, my children, work, church, and pleasures?

## SATAN IN MY LIFE?

We often ask, "What is God doing in my life?" That question is needed. But let's not be fooled into thinking that Satan is dead or no longer active. He is at work. The rebuke that Jesus leveled against Peter included a very definite reference to an evil and destructive being. Jesus spoke of Satan's presence throughout his ministry. If he existed in Peter's life, he will be present in yours. I know he functions in my world. In fact, I suspect that the spiritual warfare that the apostle Paul speaks about in Ephesians 6 is on steroids here in Washington. The "Mr. Rulers" of our culture need to acknowledge that there is a malevolent presence in this world. The New Testament describes him as a "roaring lion," out to devour whomever he chooses. C.S. Lewis provides helpful insights regarding the reality of the demonic in his book *The Screwtape Letters*.[8] Peter seemed justified in his observation and conclusion regarding Jesus in Matthew 16; yet, his thinking and words represented raw evil and, at its core, was in concert with Satan's schemes. I need to regularly ask what raw evil and sin is crouching at my door, left there by Satan? We must be in touch with whatever will tempt us to offend the Savior and his redeeming work.

What present and dangerous schemes are being directed at you and me from Satan? For Mr. Ruler, it might be a bad case of self-righteousness and pride. It could be a serious epidemic of lust or just plain discontentment. Addiction? Complaining and whining? Lacking a genuine display of the "fruit of the spirit"? Arrogance? Egotism? If Satan tormented Jesus and church leaders like Peter and Paul, he will not hesitate to go after you or me.

Often we deceive ourselves. We may have great intentions and believe our pursuits are wholesome, helpful, and honoring to God, and yet, in the end, offend him. Our real agenda is self-exaltation. This is when we need to die to self. The only true way of dying to self is to hear Jesus' rebuke regarding our narcissism and ask him to not only forgive us, but to enable us to think and live in concert with him and his way of death.

The scriptures speak about the "sting of death." Death is painful and hideous. Isn't it odd that Jesus asks us to think about our relationship with him in that context? To understand what it means for us to embrace him with our entire self takes such thinking. Doing so means daily owning the addiction, seeing what it does to us and to those we love, and also seeing how it impacts our worship and service to our Lord. In such a posture of repentance we cry out to Jesus for help.

# CHAPTER 7

# FASHION

V iolence and uncertainty dominated South Africa during
the time it became our family's home in 1993. The ANC
and the Inkatha Freedom Party, in a country of some 40
million people, regularly unleashed revulsion and hate toward each
other as a means of positioning themselves for political power. I
remember one cold morning reading the following entry in the
Johannesburg Star: "Thousands more South Africans have died
violently since 1990 than were sacrificed by the United States in
nearly 10 years of war in Vietnam's killing fields…. In less than
three-and a-half years in South Africa 52,800 people have died
violently."

These figures may seem scanty compared to the number of lives
lost in Bosnia. Well over 110,000 (perhaps as many as 200,000)

Muslims, Croats, and Serbs perished in the fight for control and supremacy after the dismantling of the Soviet Union.[9] In 1994 the Rwandan Genocide horrified the world once again. During a hundred days in Rwanda, at least 500,000 ethnic Tutsis and thousands of moderate Hutus were executed. Some report the total death figure as over 800,000.[10]

Were these brief periods in history unique in the world-class competition for hate and violent deaths? Hardly. The previously-mentioned figures pale significantly when compared to the 125 million who perished at the hands of world leaders famished for power and domination in the first half of the 20th century.[11]

The degree of evil unleashed in the world today by certain heads of state and those who serve them does not surprise me. What arguments exist to think that future leaders will be different?

Our world's distinctive leadership "fashion"—attitudes, words, and behaviors, defined in part by animosity and forms of destruction—is addictive. Dignity and grace rarely appear in a world whose leaders pursue power by any means. Life is destroyed, figuratively and, at times, literally, to obtain dominance and personal happiness. Many are oriented toward annihilating political opponents to obtain control in Washington. Why is this the norm? Why spend time assassinating an opponent's character and party instead of communicating beliefs and healthy policies? Why not work for change and progress without elevating your reputation? Those who occupy the seats of influence and rule the world tend to display fashions that serve themselves only.

## ALTERNATIVE

Radically different from the more popular worldly way, a New Testament letter instructed the Christians in Colossae to, "clothe yourselves with compassion, kindness, humility, gentleness and patience" (Colossians 3:12). This letter reflects well what Jesus spelled out in his distinct "fashion alternative" in the fifth chapter of the Gospel of Matthew:

> Blessed are the poor in spirit, for theirs is the kingdom of heaven.
>
> Blessed are those who mourn, for they will be comforted.
>
> Blessed are the meek, for they will inherit the earth.
>
> Blessed are those who hunger and thirst for righteousness, for they will be filled.
>
> Blessed are the merciful, for they will be shown mercy.
>
> Blessed are the pure in heart, for they will see God.
>
> Blessed are the peacemakers, for they will be called sons of God.
>
> **Matthew 5:1-9**

The world's fashion brand promotes self at the expense of others. It comes in varying styles and sizes. The instrument of choice usually starts as words transformed into directives and policies. Even what may seem healthy at first may later reveal itself to have been dangerously harmful. No wonder there is so much cynicism in Washington! The fashion of Jesus is fundamentally different.

The Beatitudes are Jesus' prescription for authentic happiness and satisfaction in life. His sermon accents true character and temperament. In some sense, there is a progression in the list. You cannot have the second attribute without the first. Opposition to the fashion of self-promotion and preservation creates internal conflict. There will be tension. The nature of Jesus' fashion can be divided into various categories: who we are, how we respond to others, and, how our world responds to us.

## REDEFINING **SELF**

Poverty characterized much of the world in Jesus' day, and the same sadly is true in these most modern of times, two millennia later. The World Bank located near the White House has the stated mission of a world free of poverty. The Bank noted that in 2013 more than ten percent of the world lived on less than $1.90 a day.[12] We have never been successful in ridding the globe of hunger. The war on poverty continues. My travels to Haiti, South Africa, and India bear this out. Multitudes live in crude housing and often go without meals. Depressing numbers of children have little or no hope. Poverty or "poor" are not positive terms in most cases. As noted earlier in this book, no one wants poverty for themselves or their loved ones.

One exception is found here in Jesus' sermon where it is the perfect choice. Jesus' use of the term poor sheds light on the true nature of our souls. He wants his listeners to focus on their depraved natures, their sin. We tend to think of ourselves more highly than is warranted. This results in arrogance, pride, and a judgmental attitude toward our world. The person who rightly sees his or her standing before God thinks differently. As the apostle Paul says in Romans 3:23, "They have fallen short of the glory of God." They have nothing of value to offer him. Only when we admit our spiritual poverty will we see our need of his grace, and mercy. We are helpless and without hope, longing for truth and integrity. Yet like Mr. Ruler we are not sure where to look for the answer. Do we see ourselves as needy and unsuccessful in searching for what will satisfy? If we see our poverty, we will live in a state of lament.

It may seem odd to many, including Christians, to pursue and embrace a life of mourning. Follow Jesus and look depressed? That message is unlikely to fill your church—not by itself. As a pastor I have sat with friends over the years, shedding tears with those who have experienced the loss of a spouse, parent, or child. Proper grief in the context of Jesus' Sermon on the Mount is not about experiencing physical pain, loss of a loved one, or wounded pride. It is the woeful state of one who knows his or her poverty of spirit. King David understood and experienced such mourning when confronted with his sin by the prophet Nathan after committing adultery and murder. Those who adopt the fashion of Jesus will experience a permanent degree of discomfort. The presence of soul pain because of what we truly deserve is critical for any who follow Christ. It is a blessing to be characterized as one who laments over sin. Such a state leaves us needy and famished for the gospel and grace. It is a gift to be longing and desiring for more.

## CHANGE IS NOT **AN OPTION?**

What does it mean for a person to hunger for true change politically? Instead of pursuing the destruction of a political opponent's character or of using others to promote one's career, one champions truth and interacts with grace and decency. Perhaps such radical behavior would not rate worthy of a news story, but it should. We think and act dysfunctionally. This fashion chapter defines what transforms dysfunction. Our "wanting" dispositions and addictions to self need the complete overhaul that Jesus defined as righteousness. This spiritual and moral integrity cannot be accomplished on one's own. To be righteous means that we conform perfectly to the law and will of God in every thought, word and deed. We always sing in tune. A person who does not have knowledge of God's law will have God's standard written on his or her heart and will be held to that standard (Romans 2:14-15). Most know and admit that life has left them guilty and defeated.

The person who lacks righteousness and owns his or her neediness will seek after the righteousness found only in Jesus. Paul speaks about this benefit in his letter to the Church in Rome. "… This righteousness from God comes through faith in Jesus Christ to all who believe" (Romans 3:22). Our faith in the Savior transforms our standing before a holy God. It also transforms our very being. At the same time, we daily and imperfectly face temptations, deviating from our Lord's will. For this reason we humbly seek the righteousness of another: Jesus, the Christ.

According to Jesus' sermon, those who long for the righteousness of Christ obtain a pure heart. This singleness of heart, honesty with no hidden or selfish motive, is what concerns Jesus. While outwardly giving the appearance of living in conformity to God's will, within our very being we may disregard his will. Remember, this is the concern expressed to the disciples in Mark's gospel:

For it is from within, out of a person's heart, that evil thoughts come—sexual immorality, theft, murder, adultery, greed, malice, deceit, lewdness, envy, slander, arrogance and folly.

**Mark 7:21,22**

The person who has the right heart desires to please and worship God in spirit and in truth and to love him completely. He or she understands what it means to depend upon him and obtain and maintain the heart's immutable focus. Such a heart is obtained through faith in Christ, not in self.

An additional trait redefines self. Those who are poor in spirit, brokenhearted, and hungering for righteousness are meek. There is a lack of malice, resentment, and bitterness. There is no self–righteousness in the presence of others. The apostle Paul, speaking of Jesus in Philippians 2, informs us that we should have the same attitude as Jesus, who humbled himself by taking on the nature of a servant, freely giving his life for others.

## WORLD

How should those who wear Jesus' attire impact the world? Humility, a sense of sin, and the need for forgiveness invite others to consider the gospel. An absence of arrogance and self-righteousness is very attractive. Washington and other power centers feed off the need to be popular, correct, and powerful. Does the world know how to view a leader who lacks arrogance? Treating an opponent with decency and fairness while not elevating self may invite abuse and ridicule. But this definitely will cause many to take a second look at what you really are about. And in that second look, instead of you, they might see Jesus.

This posture of humility will view the offenses of others differently. When we wear the fashion of Jesus, we do not demand justice from those who offend us while expecting mercy for our own offenses. Those who have received the mercy of God will desire to show compassion to others. They will have a gracious spirit. Do we show mercy only to those who have showered us with kindness and generosity? Jesus says, "If you love those who love you, what reward will you get? Are not even the tax collectors doing that?" (Matthew 5:46).

No, the merciful are those who have been offended and treat the offender with the benevolence that comes from the spirit of grace. To be clear, this does not mean we are justice-blind. We should work to address the injustices of our communities and world. We possibly may pursue righting wrongs knowing that the matter, if not addressed, will place a community in danger. Yet we address wrongs with a gracious and redemptive spirit—not in self-righteousness or for personal gain. When our hearts, our soul's hungers and dispositions, reflect the gospel's transforming influence, we will distinctively impact our community and world. The consequences of godly humility and mercy will be evident.

As much as we would like to see world harmony, we live in times characterized by conflict and pure malevolence. In more personal areas, we see the need for harmony within our relationships. The family today often hungers for reconciliation and peace. No one needs to rehearse the depressing annual broken marriage statistics. We must make the sacrifice to pursue healthy relationships in the home regardless of the career cost. It must happen. Children and marriages often take second place as they are abandoned for career pursuits, leaving loneliness and, at times, unresolved conflict and bitterness.[13] Children who are reared in broken homes are at a disadvantage in a dysfunctional broken world. In many cases the family needs someone who has learned the way of making and maintaining peace. If home, the most sacred place in our lives, is consumed with conflict and tension, how can we expect our communities, schools and nation to be any different? Our modern and advanced world needs biblical peacemakers. Lives transformed by Jesus have been granted the greatest peace that man could desire. Christians are called to actively engage in the work of reconciliation. Such work is possible because we ourselves have been reconciled to God through Christ. Paul makes this point in 2 Corinthians 5, "All this is from God, who reconciled us to himself through Christ and gave us the ministry of reconciliation," (v. 18). Our world of turmoil hungers for those who are making peace that both reflects and is empowered by the gospel.

# PERSECUTED

Living in a Christ-like fashion may result in an outpouring of hate. Jesus never promises the absence of conflict. He continues in his sermon to describe life when lived out under his terms.

> Blessed are those who are persecuted because of righteousness, for theirs is the kingdom of heaven.
>
> Blessed are you when people insult you, persecute you and falsely say all kinds of evil against you because of me.
>
> Rejoice and be glad, because great is your reward in heaven, for in the same way they persecuted the prophets who were before you.
>
> **Matthew 5:10-12**

It sounds odd that Jesus would say there is blessing in being treated poorly. Who wants persecution? Contempt may occur in the home, the workplace, the political arena, or from friends. In some parts of the world the persecution will come directly from those in power.

This is not persecution for social, environmental, political, or economic reasons, but because of righteousness—Jesus' righteousness. The fashion of Jesus is centered on him. He is the one who, through the Spirit and Word, works in our lives and enables us to wear his fashion well.

The apostles learned first-hand what experiencing the world's wrath meant, as we read in the book of Acts. Followers of Jesus accepted the hardships as a form of identity. The writer of Hebrews says it well: "You sympathized with those in prison and joyfully accepted the confiscation of your property, because you knew that you yourselves had better and lasting possessions." (Hebrews 10:34).

# IMPACT

Following Jesus transforms individual character and, by its very nature, impacts the world. Jesus calls us salt and light (Matthew 5:13-16). A flavor enhancer, salt also is used as a preservative. Our world deteriorates in every form imaginable: socially, politically, morally, economically, physically, and spiritually. We all fade and deteriorate. Many institutions, including the church, suffer various forms of decay.

Numerous Christian denominations that once stood for the essentials of historic Christianity (basic truths of the Bible) no longer hold to Jesus' way.[14] Believing that the Scripture and its gospel are irrelevant and outdated diminishes and numbs the conscience. Clearly this disappointing change impacts our communities and country. The salt has lost its value.

The people of God are for the people of the world. They cannot afford to stay withdrawn, mute or unengaged. Those wearing the godly fashion that Jesus taught will draw the attention of the world as they live Jesus-dominated lives. This influence needs to be more than occasional. It should take place in every sphere of life; yes, especially in the 24/7 political sphere.

The additional influence of Jesus' fashion will not only be to preserve what is good, but to provide positive direction. Light is needed to guide and direct. It removes fear and brings comfort and the hope of heaven. It is Jesus who is the light of the world in the supreme sense.

> In him was life, and that life was the light of men.
> The light shines in the darkness, but the darkness
> has not understood it."
>
> **John 1:4-5**

The recipients of light have the privilege of transmitting it to their world. The fashion of Jesus is more than an ideology or educational system; in fact, it is more than a message. The fashion of Jesus is centered upon his person. He is the only one who works in our lives and enables us to wear his fashion well.

The way of Jesus challenges the "Mr. Rulers" and the rest of us with the gospel. Not only does that gospel give us future hope, it also changes our ailing hearts, minds and behavior. The need for such transformation here in Washington is great. Those who believe the change will be political will wait for eternity. It will never come through political means. The needed transformation comes through a change in hearts.

# CHAPTER 8

# INFLUENCE

I t was a warm autumn day that afforded my friend and me a pleasant walk along a row of shops in Sofia, Bulgaria. He and his family had made the former communist country their home. As we approached a small grocery, he told me that he found some of their store policies a bit odd. When he had started shopping at the store, the shelves carried Oreo Cookies, which he would frequently purchase for himself and for his family. Over time he noticed that the store was no longer stocking them. When he asked why, the owner explained that Oreos had become too popular and, therefore, took a great deal of time and effort to supply. The storeowner preferred to stock items that did not sell well. That explanation made no sense to my friend or to me.

The grocer's logic is confusing to anyone who has lived in a free society. Any item that sells well is frequently restocked because it brings in more revenue. The grocer in Sofia typifies a nation that has followed the influential policies of Marxism. Such policies cause a serious economic distortion. If you carry products that sell, you must work harder to keep them on the shelves. In the former Soviet Union there was no reward for additional work. Communism has greatly influenced significant parts of the world for decades.

Eight years later I worshiped in a small house church in Beijing, China. These believers met weekly for prayer and fellowship in their nation's capital. China has remained communist since the late 1940's. As we drank tea after worship, a middle-aged woman shared her faith story; she had come to know Jesus under the ideology of Marxism. "I received nothing over the course of my life from communism," she said, "but Christ has given me everything!" Beijing offered me many opportunities to hear from new friends how the gospel had transformed their lives. Often there had been an acquaintance whose life had been notably transformed by Christ. Even in that context the gospel message prevailed. The presence of the gospel will challenge and transform individuals, friends and nations.

The 18th-century English politician William Wilberforce believed that his faith should not remain private. Best known for pursuing the long process of moving his nation to abolish the slave trade, he lived life in a way that altered the world in which God had placed him.[15] In some ways the influential Wilberforce reminds me of a man named Daniel, spoken of in the Old Testament. I believe that many who work here in Washington could learn a lot from this man who lived some 2,600 years ago.

Daniel, along with his three friends, Hananiah, Mishael, and Azariah, had been forced to leave their home in Jerusalem and serve King Nebuchadnezzar in Babylonia. Young and talented, they were placed in a three-year education program to prepare them in the disciplines needed to serve the king. The king's food they were required to eat, however, was forbidden to Israelites, so Daniel asked their official supervisor, Ashpenaz, if he and the other three could have a diet of vegetables and water.

The first chapter of Daniel provides the following details:

> ...but the official told Daniel, 'I am afraid of my lord the king, who has assigned your food and drink. Why should he see you looking worse than the other young men your age? The king would then have my head because of you.' Daniel then said to the guard whom the chief official had appointed over Daniel, Hananiah, Mishael and Azariah, 'Please test your servants for ten days: Give us nothing but vegetables to eat and water to drink. Then compare our appearance with that of the young men who eat the royal food, and treat your servants in accordance with what you see.' So, he agreed to this and tested them for ten days. At the end of the ten days they looked healthier and better nourished than any of the young men who ate the royal food. So the guard took away their choice food and the wine they were to drink and gave them vegetables instead.
>
> **Daniel 1:10-16**

Daniel found himself in a place that was not his home, serving a ruler that was not his king, and required to eat offensive food. He and his friends daily faced challenges to faith and life in a strange land. Living in a foreign culture is difficult, and even more so when forced to do so against your will. This prophet, as Jesus refers to him (Matthew 24:15), demonstrates important truths about living out our faith in a world usually inimical to the gospel.

## CONVICTIONS AND **PRINCIPLES**

Why did Daniel and his friends find the diet offensive? Who in his right mind would complain when given the food from a king's chef and kitchen? Yet, the provisions created a grave predicament for Daniel. Why? Was it an issue of violating the Levitical Law? Was the meat from unclean animals? C.F. Keil, in his Old Testament commentary, points out that the issue had nothing to do with Jewish dietary requirements. The concern was that eating the required food was to participate in the worship of the foreign gods.[16]

According to the Babylonians, the primary purpose of man was to serve the gods. This service was done by priests dressing as gods and providing daily gifts of food at the temples. The temple personnel included different types of priests, singers, prostitutes, prophets, and diviners. Some of the activities were designed to ward off evil spirits.

For Daniel, to eat the meat and drink the wine that had been offered was synonymous with participating in the worship of the Babylonian gods. Daniel would not. Yet, if you are under the rule of another what option do you have unless you are willing to die?

Whose rule are we under? What governs our thoughts and actions? What influences us? How well do we discern God's will? Daniel knew God and his Word and was determined to obey. What a great dilemma for these Jews. One cannot have a godly influence on the world without biblical convictions that will not be compromised.

## GRACIOUS AND CIVIL

Daniel was diplomatic. Knowing what was right, he addressed the issue of having to consume both food and drink. Given the circumstances, I might have responded in a more straightforward and self-righteous manner. But that was not Daniel's approach. He was not arrogant or rude. He assessed the circumstances and looked for a way to work through his dilemma without causing a revolt or losing his head. Daniel asked for permission to replace the king's food. God caused the official to show favor, as he listened with sympathy. Daniel then made a proposal that the chief official could relate to and, possibly, grant: Replace the king's food with vegetables and water for ten days and then make the evaluation. After the ten-day trial, the official was more than impressed. Wow, these guys looked great! I like how Old Testament scholar E.J. Young refers to what took place: "To accomplish this end, Daniel displays no fanaticism or rudeness, but candidly states his purpose to the chief chamberlain and asks his help. At this point, as throughout his life, Daniel exhibits himself as a true gentleman. He never yields in devotion to principle, but he does not permit devotion to principle to serve as a cloak for rudeness or fanaticism. He was a true hero of the Faith."[17]

It takes a great deal of patience and wisdom to respond as Daniel did. It is so easy to be rude. Daniel understood the pragmatic world in which Ashpenaz lived; Daniel had to communicate within that understanding. If one did not follow the king's order, he was killed. Daniel did not say as a way of arguing his case, "This is the Word of God." That had no meaning to Ashpenaz. Daniel spoke to him in the language he knew and terms that he could consider. It made a significant difference. But something else also needs to be considered.

## GOD'S PRESENCE

Had God abandoned Daniel, his friends and the other Israelites? Are we not tempted under stressful times to conclude this? Continuing the account in the first chapter we read of the nature of God's presence.

> To these four young men God gave knowledge and understanding of all kinds of literature and learning. And Daniel could understand visions and dreams of all kinds. At the end of the time set by the king to bring them in, the chief official presented them to Nebuchadnezzar. The king talked with them, and he found none equal to Daniel, Hananiah, Mishael and Azariah; so they entered the king's service. In every matter of wisdom and understanding about which the king questioned them, he found them ten times better than all the magicians and enchanters in his whole kingdom. And Daniel remained there until the first year of King Cyrus.
>
> **(Daniel 1:17-21)**

Daniel and his friends experienced God's presence in amazing ways, as indicated in the passage. Perhaps Daniel could have lived in bitterness toward God for placing him in a foreign country, but, clearly, he did not. We are informed that the Lord was with Daniel and had blessed him and his friends in many ways, both physically and intellectually. It was God who caused the official to show favor and sympathy to Daniel. It was God who gave the four men knowledge and understanding of all kinds of literature and learning. To live life in God's presence is not only to be changed by God through the gospel, but also to influence the world around you as one who has been transformed by it.

What does it mean to live in the presence of God when living in the world?

We are to live knowing that nothing takes place outside of God's control and purpose. It is not uncommon for Christians to live as though their faith is based more on the past rather than the present. It is important that we do not forget all that God has done for us in Jesus. The Savior is alive. He is not too busy or asleep. He is always a "present help." The psalmist puts it this way:

> Where can I go from your Spirit? Where can I flee from your presence? If I go up to the heavens, you are there; if I make my bed in the depths, you are there. If I rise on the wings of the dawn, if I settle on the far side of the sea, even there your hand will guide me, your right hand will hold me fast.
>
> **Psalm 139:7-10**

Within the first year of moving to Washington in 2003 I met Michael Schwartz who, at the time, was chief of staff for Senator Tom Coburn. Michael previously headed a number of non-profits and was best known as an advocate for unborn children and their mothers. Over the years, until his death in 2013, he became a close friend. We spent a lot of time together, allowing me to witness the great influence he had upon others. He loved God, his family and work. He devoted himself to the study of scripture and prayer. I know few who were as loyal to a boss as Michael. If I stopped by his office on the first floor of the Russell Senate office Building, he was often advising and counseling those who sought his wisdom. People were drawn to him.

I witnessed a display of Christ-like character, regardless of the circumstances. When his health failed him, and he knew he was going to die, I saw how well he lived out his last days, serving others as he had always done. In my opinion, Michael was a modern-day Daniel.

For those who only know how to make demands and have them immediately met, as we assume was the case for Mr. Ruler, Daniel's example is a challenge. Mr. Ruler was very much in control of his life. He did not need to submit to others. He was a man of influence. His reward was to have others join him in self-worship. When confronted with the cost of following Jesus, he would not compromise, nor did he attempt to bargain. He went away cheerless because of the great idol that persistently dictated orders which he obeyed: Serve well your self. We do not know the rest of his story. We can only hope that in time he surrendered to Christ and became a gospel influence to those who knew him. Men and women who reflect the spiritual integrity and character of Daniel are what Washington and other cities need.

# CHAPTER 9

# LEADERSHIP

My Father, a plumber, instilled in me a formula for leadership. He was a man of integrity, confident and direct. Despite having little formal education beyond high school, he understood the value of being a visionary and gathering the right people around him to accomplish desired goals. He won trust and loyalty from those who knew him. They took him at his word, never doubting the integrity of his statements. In time my father became a successful builder and developer.

What I witnessed in his work was what I saw at home. Sadly, as a child I dishonored him at times; my dishonor was never warranted. In each season of his life and career, he modeled the positive characteristics of a godly leader. I believe there are leaders in Washington like this; I also know that many others would not qualify.

Perhaps King David's children thought the same of their father, one of the greatest leaders the nation of Israel has ever known. King David's formula for leadership has been studied carefully. English historian, Paul Johnson, noted this: "David became the most successful and popular king Israel ever had, the archetype king and ruler, so that for more than 2,000 years after his death Jews saw his reign as a golden age."[18] (By no means was his rule without serious challenges, however. Johnson writes that it was always precarious.) David's greatness often has been judged by his accomplishments; but, are accomplishments the truest measure of greatness? Is there more to the formula? Should we look for other attributes as well? What qualities are essential for a leader here in Washington? Are the main goals to be pragmatic, to "just get the job done," to check the latest CNN polls, to please the constituents? Or to lead with integrity? Does one's home or personal life inform or impact one's work as a leader? Should a leader be autonomous or dependent? Does a leader need to communicate openly, be transparent, or be secretive in his dealings? Does it matter if a leader is dictatorial, or should he or she lead with sensitivity to others, building consensus? Does it matter how a leader deals with the stranger, refugee, and alien? How does a leader confront failure, resolve conflict, or persevere in hard times? Is there value in a leader's ability to respect those who differ from and oppose him?

The historic account of David's life and rule addresses many of these questions. Consider a few aspects of his leadership.

# DEPENDENCE

King David was childlike. He was not autonomous. At the core he was not self-directed, self-sufficient, or self-governing. David was dependent. You say, "This cannot be!" How could anyone who has a 3,000-year-old reputation as a great king be anything but strong in sovereignty? But consider the record. He wanted to build the most significant physical structure in all of history, the Temple. Toward the end of his life, he had to deal with the reality that his dream and desire would not come true. Through the prophet Nathan, God made clear that David's son, Solomon, would build the temple. Why? David was unqualified because he was a warrior, a man who had shed blood (1 Chronicles 28:3). If David had been more autonomous, he would have acted like Cain who became angry when God would not accept his offering. Instead of submitting to God, Cain turned against him, lacked repentance, and murdered his brother. David, on the other hand, submitted to God's will and looked for ways to serve his son, Solomon, even though he would never see the temple built. His assistance took the form of collecting the resources that would be necessary to build the holy structure. When the capital campaign was completed, David gathered the community together and spoke these words:

> Praise be to you, O LORD, God of our father Israel, from everlasting to everlasting. Yours, O LORD, is the greatness and the power and the glory and the majesty and the splendor, for everything in heaven and earth is yours. Yours, O LORD, is the kingdom; you are exalted as head over all. Wealth and honor come from you; you are

the ruler of all things. In your hands are strength and power to exalt and give strength to all.

**1 Chronicles 29:10-12**

These are the words of a man who understood that he was not sovereign. His position as king was a gift from God. The resources used to carry out his rule did not belong to him. Any structure built or battle won was not a result of his own wisdom or power. The kingdom belonged to God. David was a steward. Everything he owned and accomplished, he credited to the Lord, his God. David depended on the eternal king.

Such leadership is difficult to find in our day. Sometimes faith is used to obtain leadership, but abandoned once the power position has been attained.

## MORAL **FAILURE**

History has never hidden the truth regarding David's moral failures. The ethical integrity of a leader is not ignored even today, when faith is often ridiculed or absent. Every year, the media crave details about accusations of unethical behavior by members of Congress or the administration. The law written upon the hearts of all of Adam's children continues to show itself. There are still standards of behavior even though the lines may seem blurred. Truth in David's day was not fuzzy. Lines were clearly drawn. Even for a king the Law given by Moses was not optional. Yet, one evening, David ignored that Law.

Sleep evaded King David one night. Perhaps the Israeli-Ammonite conflict weighed heavily on his mind. Weary, he was sexually tempted. From the rooftop of his palace he could see an extremely attractive woman – the wife of another man – bathing. Her name: Bathsheba. Was it only in the light of a full moon that his eyes could be satisfied? Certainly, this was not the first time? Why did he not find satisfaction in his own wives? Before the evening was over, he had her brought to his royal chambers and slept with her as if she were his wife. Upon learning that she was pregnant, David believed the matter could best be handled by arranging for the murder of Bathsheba's husband. Successful in his plan, David believed the concern was settled. He was wrong.

Eventually the prophet Nathan confronted the king. David then acknowledged what he had attempted to hide. Some details of his confession are found in Psalm 51, which reveals the heart of a king who saw himself as a God-offender. From this he learned afresh what it meant to be a recipient of God's grace and forgiveness. To me, this is essential in a leader.

A leader who does not see his or her weaknesses and sins is a fool. Such arrogance is the perfect condition for failure. The leader becomes judgmental and hardhearted. A leader who concurs with the psalmist, however, will demonstrate a posture of humility and dependence upon the true King. Such a leader will view others with grace and kindness, since he himself has received grace and kindness.

At the end of David's life, he prepared his son Solomon, whose mother was Bathsheba, for kingship:

> When the time drew near for David to die, he gave a charge to Solomon his son. "I am about to go the way of all the earth," he said. "So be strong, show yourself a man, and observe what the LORD your God requires: Walk in his ways,

and keep his decrees and commands, his laws and
requirements...."

**1 Kings 2:1-3**

David knew well the importance and consequences of his
words. He was not independent, but reliant upon God. He knew
the joy and pleasure of observing God's requirements. He also
knew the pain of ignoring them. Such a view makes for a powerful
and healthy leader.

## FAITH EXPRESSED

A few years ago, some politicos assumed that a serious can-
didate for office would keep his religion to himself. This is not so.
After the 2004 election I attended a number of forums in Washington, D.C., hosted by the party that had not fared well during the
elections. As expected, the party members bemoaned their losses.
The purpose of the gatherings was to review what had gone wrong
and to discuss how to make things right the next time around. The
exit polls had seemed to characterize the party as lacking values
and faith. They deplored this characterization.

I did not know the particulars of the party member's beliefs.
But since that gathering, I have noticed that candidates for both
parties (quite unlike Western Europe) make a point of speaking
about religion. Over the past few years, much has been written
about faith and leadership. Is it wise to use faith as a means of
gaining a political position.? When is it appropriate to openly
express your faith views?

While these questions may be useful for those seeking office
in the United States, and perhaps elsewhere in the world, they

would have seemed strange for Israel's head of state in 10th-century, B.C. Faith was not a private matter. On occasion King David expressed his love and devotion to God by dancing, celebrating before the Lord. His time and circumstances were different, you may say. True. David was king of a theocracy. But, certainly, there are appropriate expressions of faith for today's leaders.

Near the end of his life, David gathered the leaders of the nation together and celebrated. Why? God had blessed his efforts to secure the needed resources to build the temple, which he would not see. David's worship follows:

> The people rejoiced at the willing response of their leaders, for they had given freely and wholeheartedly to the LORD. David the king also rejoiced greatly.
>
> David praised the LORD in the presence of the whole assembly, saying, "Praise be to you, O LORD, God of our father Israel, from everlasting to everlasting."
>
> **1 Chronicles 29:9-10**

Yes, there are times for a leader of faith to have private worship; there are also times when it is appropriate to go public. The Oklahoma City Bombing and 9-11 were two occasions when leaders had the opportunity to express their faith and allow the community to join with them. Days after the bombing in Oklahoma City, thousands gathered for a time of worship at the invitation of Mayor Ron Norick and Governor Frank Keating. The place was so packed that I was not able to enter the large facility. The gathering included governors from neighboring states as well as President Clinton and Dr. Billy Graham. Without question, the Lord was exalted. What about when other tragedies occur? Or an inauguration? Or the funeral for a head of state? Or recognition of the completion of a project? Expose one's faith as a leader? Why not?

Faith is terribly tricky for leaders in today's world. If done for political gain, it will be obvious. Speaking of our faith in God should be done for only one reason: God's glory. All public expressions from the lips of a leader must be done in the humility of one who grieves his or her offense to God and embraces the gospel.

# CHAPTER 10

# REST

Soon after Congress declared war on Japan and Germany, Winston Churchill spent weeks discussing future plans with President Roosevelt and his advisers in Washington, D.C. The meetings were so draining that one of Roosevelt's advisors, Harry Hopkins, checked himself into the Washington Naval Hospital for a week of bed rest. Exhausted, on January 5th Churchill accepted an offer to spend a few days re-energizing at a home in Pompano Beach, Florida. Historian William Manchester wrote:

"Upon arrival, [Churchill] headed straight way for the beach, where he reveled in the warm ocean waters, and swam about, naked, until somebody spotted the large shark." Being warned, "Churchill stayed put pawing happily about."[19]

Who doesn't enjoy relaxing, stretched out on the sun-bleached shores overlooking the Florida waters? Picture the scene: a good book and a cool drink, interrupted only by an occasional dip in cool, refreshing waters. Sure, it is not for everybody. Your preferred leisure menu may vary from mine. Perhaps you prefer a game of golf or a Caribbean cruise. Most know what they want when pursuing a break. Some find work so intoxicating that it is hard to stop, but most people want the shortest possible workweek and longer holidays. Does it matter what we believe about the relationship between work and rest? Does the way a person slows down and stop say anything about his personality, her view of life, or faith?

Scripture speaks about the importance and nature of work. The beginning pages of Genesis deal with divine and human labor. God is introduced in his work of creation, followed by the call for Adam and Eve to work in a Mesopotamian garden and build a family. Many characters throughout the Bible are identified by their careers: David herded sheep before becoming a king, the Excellent Wife of Proverbs 31 owned her own business, the apostle Peter was a fisherman, and Lydia dealt in purple cloth. Many biblical passages praise work by warning against idleness:

> I went past the field of the sluggard, past the vineyard of the man who lacks judgment; thorns had come up everywhere, the ground was covered with weeds, and the stone wall was in ruins. I applied my heart to what I observed and learned a lesson from what I saw: A little sleep, a little slumber, a little folding of the hands to rest-and poverty will come on you like a bandit and scarcity like an armed man.
>
> **Proverbs 24:30-34**

Jesus warned his followers about the importance of labor with the Parable of the Talents in Matthew 25. The Apostle Paul expressed concerns regarding those who refuse to work:

> ... keep away from every brother who is idle and does not live according to the teaching you received from us.
>
> 2 Thessalonians 3:6

Working hard is a virtue in the Bible. I suspect that the Mr. Rulers of the world tend to fall into the category of workaholics. Often their toil, at the expense of everything else in life, feeds their idol of self. They need no instruction on the importance of applying themselves to their blossoming careers. But I am also certain that their schedules include room for leisure and refreshment. Mr. Ruler's Jewish culture would have been shaped by the regular absence of labor taught in the Old Testament. The question for us today is not whether we ever put work aside, but what is the nature of those vacations? How do the Scriptures guide us in being still? I am not talking about the Lord's Day or the Sabbath, per se. I am referring to a form of rest that King David addresses in the Psalms:

> The Lord is my shepherd I shall lack nothing, he makes me lie down in green pastures, he leads me beside the quiet waters, he restores my soul. He guides me in paths of righteousness for his name sake. Even though I walk through the valley of the

shadow of death, I will fear no evil, for you are with me; your rod and staff, they comfort me.

Psalm 23:1-4

This kind of respite is a window into one's understanding of the gospel and one's relationship with God. The priority and character of our rest shows us something of what we believe about the stewardship of our resources and time.

# DIVINE

King David lived a dynamic life around 900 years before the birth of Jesus. He grew up in a hard-working family that raised sheep and other livestock. He knew how to protect himself from the forces of danger. David's upbringing proved to be a perfect nursery for becoming a warrior king where he would often experience great difficulties in both public and private life. A well-known leader, he had much power and influence. Yet, as indicated in Psalm 23, he knew rest well. In many respects, he would have been an ideal mentor for Mr. Ruler.

The concept of rest is divine. In fact, God created humans to taste and enjoy it. Our desire and need for it is certainly not a result of the Fall, our past offense to God. God set the stage for the pleasure of a break when he spent the seventh day of history's first week enjoying what he had accomplished on the prior six days. Yes, this was foundational for the establishment of the Sabbath, and also informative regarding a model for life—the way we live throughout the course of the day. If God, in the midst of creating and governing the universe, sees the need to stop and reflect shouldn't we also?

Real rest is pursued in the context of worship, because when we are still, we acknowledge God's presence in the busyness of our days and weeks. David says it is the Lord, his shepherd, who leads him to green pastures and still waters. The gracious, promise-keeping God who is King of kings and Lord of lords also is the God who gives breaks. It is only proper to acknowledge him and thank him for this needed gift.

## DIRECTED

Some believe that although God created and governs the universe, he does not impose himself upon creation; that is, he is passive. What happens in history is the result of people living in absolute freedom as they respond to random events. Yet, the gospel informs us that Jesus came to a world that did not receive him and died for those who rejected him. He acted with no one's permission. The gospel also informs us that those who embrace his grace and love do so by his Spirit who performs heart surgery on those who are in rebellion. All this to say that he does not wait for us to make the first move. Without our permission he accomplished his work of redemption. David's words are an acknowledgement of sovereign direction in time of rest. "He makes me lie down …He leads me..." (v. 2). Jesus is not a passive shepherd who simply provides a brochure of leisure options as the Ritz-Carlton concierge does. He is all about guiding and directing. David saw the divine shepherd actively taking charge of his life and circumstances, even though uninvited. God knows my needs even better than I know myself. He is intimately knowledgeable about my physical, emotional, spiritual, and social needs. My work, family, pain, struggles, temptations, discomforts, and stress are well understood by the Lord. All my weariness from worry and anxiety is not strange to him. So, taking into account all that I am, he directs my life by his Word and Spirit. This divine direction includes my refreshment and leisure.

> O LORD, you have searched me and you know me. You know when I sit and when I rise; you perceive my thoughts from afar. You discern my going out and my lying down; you are familiar with all my ways. Before a word is on my tongue you know it completely, O LORD.
>
> **Psalm 139:1-4**

This is the reason the divine presence is so dangerous. In my rest, I am given permission to be still and observe who I am and all that is happening in my life. That can be hazardous for any of us. Why is such calm a potential problem? I might see the reality that my busy schedule has kept in seclusion. In my rest I will see my sin, my anxiety, and the reasons for them. When next to quiet waters, I will be confronted with my recent offenses against my wife, children, neighbor, and God himself. In that green pasture I may see just how much life I desire from my idols of self-promotion and glory-seeking. Perhaps this is why so much of our rest is in name only. We want to keep God out.

## PROVISION

What resources are needed for a season of relaxation and leisure? In the Spring of 2007, Debby and I spent a long week traveling through Puerto Rico. The getaway afforded us several days snorkeling off the remote island of Culebra. Beautiful coral reefs and colorful fish in the clear Caribbean waters mesmerized us for hours at a time. Later in the week, we enjoyed hiking in rainforest mountains on the east side of the mainland. The lush foliage and cool mountain air provided a perfect setting to enjoy the view of the valley and surrounding hills. Both the location and the ability to experience and to enjoy it were a gift.

Green pastures and quiet waters were not designed or created by man. They originated from God. It is a gift to breathe the mountain air and have strength to walk hiking paths. It is a privilege to swim in crystal waters and feel the sun's warmth on your back. True, many lack the luxuries described above. Their place of quiet may be a park, hiking path, tranquil room or back porch that affords some break from the frenzy of the week. For others, that place is a certain neighborhood sidewalk or bench to sit upon and read. It may be a time of day free from interruptions, enjoying our Lord's provisions and presence. Regardless, it is a time to reflect on God, his Word, grace, and glory. When I recognize that I am in the presence of the living God, my mind and being are transformed. In rest we are drawn to pray and voice our fears and needs to the one who has demonstrated care and comfort in Jesus.

## VALLEY

I have noted a personal, sobering reality when thinking about King David's Psalm. He refers to the "valley of the shadow of death." David knew well the hardship, suffering and death that existed in his life and world. Does this not negate all that he said in the earlier verses?

In 1993 while on sabbatical in Cape Town, South Africa, I learned that a group of terrorists had burst into a worship service

at St. James Church only a few miles away from where I was staying. It took only minutes for these gunmen to kill eleven and injure
fifty-eight of the worshipers who had gathered to sing hymns and
pray.

After our South Africa sabbatical, my family and I eventually returned home to Oklahoma City. On the morning of April
19, 1995, at 8:30, I drove past the Myriad Convention Center
in Oklahoma City. Some twelve hundred had gathered there to
pray for their community and consider the truths of the Scriptures as several spoke about the gospel. A few blocks north, at 9:02
AM, the 4,800-pound fertilizer bomb inside Timothy McVeigh's
Ryder truck was detonated reducing the Federal Building and
other structures to a pile of ruins. The death toll reached 168 with
another 500 people severely injured. People with lost limbs and
eyesight will suffer physically and emotionally for their remaining
days. How are we to make sense of such tragedy? How are we to
understand the significance of a faith community humbling themselves in prayer, only to be immediately rewarded by an act of mass
murder?

On the morning of June 17, 2015, in Washington, D.C., I
joined one hundred and forty South Carolinians gathered for a
prayer breakfast in the Kennedy Caucus Room in the Russell Senate Office Building on Capitol Hill. The Senate and House members, their staffers and other guests were greeted by a poster with
the following words from the Old Testament:

> The Spirit of the Sovereign LORD is on me,
> because the LORD has anointed me to proclaim
> good news to the poor. He has sent me to bind
> up the brokenhearted, to proclaim freedom for
> the captives and release from darkness for the

prisoners, to proclaim the year of the LORD's favor and the day of vengeance of our God, to comfort all who mourn, and provide for those who grieve in Zion— to bestow on them a crown of beauty instead of ashes, the oil of joy instead of mourning, and a garment of praise instead of a spirit of despair. They will be called oaks of righteousness, a planting of the LORD for the display of his splendor.

**Isaiah 61:1-3**

That very evening, Dylann Roof shot and killed nine members who had gathered for study and prayer at the Emanuel African Methodist Episcopal Church in Charleston, South Carolina. Those murdered were constituents of the South Carolina delegation that had met and prayed under the banner of Isaiah 61 earlier that day. The small group in Charleston, whose number was similar to the gathering of Jesus and his disciples in the upper room, had been by the still waters and in green pastures that evening. They were together in the presence of their sovereign shepherd who calls his own to rest. Why should these betrayed people consider prayer and faith of any value? How are we to make sense of Christians in worship being met with horrific tragedy?

I am not sure I know the entire answer. What I do know is that some two thousand years ago thirteen men gathered for fellowship and worship in an upper room in Palestine. After the gathering, one of them betrayed the group's leader. Within hours, the one betrayed was sentenced to death and executed as a common criminal. Why? Did David have some veiled understanding of this when he wrote about the valley of the shadow of death? We live in a very broken world in great turmoil and in need of healing. As long as we are on this side of heaven, the dark valley will remain. For that reason Jesus accepted the betrayal and its consequences. Only through his humility and bold suffering can we have true freedom from all that this fallen world will give. The circumstances met by those in Cape Town, Oklahoma City, and Charleston are confusing and seem senseless. Yet the gospel leaves us with more than confusion; it leaves us with great hope. No one knows more about entering the valley after a time besides quiet waters and green pastures than Jesus. God demonstrates his grace when he leads us beside water and grass just before we enter the dark valley. We cannot avoid the coming valley, but we can choose to be still and re-energize as a means of preparing for it.

## SATISFYING

Sometimes the pursuit of rest leaves us disappointed. The psalmist speaks of a rest that is satisfying and complete: "I shall lack nothing...He restores my soul." We cannot control the weather, the airline that loses our luggage, or the roaches in our hotel room. Sometimes we burn from too much sun, we grow frustrated by long lines at a museum, or suffer from food poisoned by the chef. Things happen that ruin our perfect holiday. We return exhausted and tired, rather than refreshed.

David speaks about a calm that restores the soul. Such rest comes from God. Divine rest is not only physical, but spiritual. Jesus says, "Come to me, all you who are weary and burdened, and I will give you rest" (Matthew 11:28). There is no refreshment comparable to what Jesus gives. He gave himself so that we would have peace and true life now, and in the future, eternal rest.

When Mr. Ruler walked away from following Jesus, he denied himself the rest for which his soul longed. I strongly suspect that what motivated him to seek Jesus was the deep desire to be at peace within his spent soul. He had to have been exhausted from being bossed around by the idols of possessions, position, and reputation. He desperately needed divine rest. But the idols would not let go of him. And he would not let go of the idols.

Do we think that by staying in control, life will be good? Until Mr. Ruler could own his weariness and see the dead end to which it was ultimately leading him, he could never appreciate or enjoy the still waters. The same is true for us. Only when we see our lives drained, will we see our need to follow Jesus. I can only imagine what Capitol Hill and 1600 Pennsylvania Avenue could be were those who labor there to seek the presence, peace, and rest of the gracious Shepherd.

# CHAPTER 11

# LOVE

ertain adjectives come readily to mind when describing people in Washington: powerful, egotistical, deceptive (immoral, cynical), selfish, narcissistic. What rarely comes to mind is the adjective "loving." Former Secretary of Defense Robert Gates once characterized the nation's capital this way: "It's always a treat to be someplace other than Washington, D.C.—the only place where, as I like to say, you can see a prominent person walking down Lover's Lane holding his own hand."[20] Washington is not characterized by real love. The city is starving for love, and perhaps has never known it since its birth as a seat of government. Washington tends to use and abuse people, leaving them exhausted.

The account of Mr. Ruler from Mark's Gospel shows an exhausted person. You recall the details: This Jewish billionaire had a hive of employees running his successful corporate pursuits. He drove a Tesla Roadster and lived in a home behind guarded iron gates that contemporaries could only dream of. When he spoke, people listened. If he showed interest in a business opportunity, venture capitalists bought into it as a winner. The world and its media were captivated by his power. Power and luxury intoxicated both them and him.

Having "the world," however, is not the same as having everything. This is clear from the sole non-business pursuit that drove this man. In his quiet moments, he was plagued by gnawing questions about his eternal future. So he asked Jesus, "What must I do to inherit eternal life?"

His approach certainly drew attention. Abandoning all sense of dignity as a societal leader, he anxiously ran to Jesus and dropped to his knees. Imagine the president of a nation doing that! The matter was urgent; Mr. Ruler had no mere business issue to broach or physical healing to plead. He was compelled by the realization that he was unprepared for his own death. Until now, everything had seemed in order; life had run according to his dictates. Is it possible that someone had been talking to him about the teachings of Jesus, and the teacher's words had troubled him?

I am sure he believed it safe to ask Jesus about this matter. He did not imagine that the response would threaten what he prized most—his power, possessions, and position. Yet Jesus' reply to the man's burning question was simultaneously inviting and confrontational. Fascinatingly, the reply contained the very thing the young ruler idolized: power. But it was power of a far superior kind. Jesus' response resonated with the power of God's love. Mark records that "Jesus looked at him and loved him." Yet that powerful, divine love challenged the ruler's own idol of human power.

"One thing you lack," the Savior said. "Go, sell everything you have, give to the poor, and you will have treasure in heaven. Then come follow me." Mark writes that the man's face fell and he departed without a word, "because he had great wealth." Then Jesus turned to his disciples and addressed them almost as if they were standing on Capitol Hill: "How hard it is for the rich to enter the kingdom of God!" (Mark 10:23)

## LOVE **NEEDED**

Mr. Ruler had come for an answer in order to quickly "fix" the problem and move on. Undoubtedly there were mergers, acquisitions and other management decisions to direct. He knew that things are easily resolved if you bring in an "expert," and there was no question that Jesus was the right man for the job!

The expert tossed out a few questions. He listed several of the Ten Commandments: Had the man kept them? Mr. Ruler nodded, "All these I have kept since I was a boy." The man knew his Bible and had respect for God's laws.

I have met others who would answer similarly; but, there is a problem when someone believes he has kept God's law. That person is not well-connected to reality. He does not know himself. Paul tells us in Romans 3:23, "All have sinned and fallen short of the glory of God." The apostle John cautions that the person who claims he has not sinned is a liar (I John 1:8-10).

It was at this point that Jesus confronted the man with his self-deception. In essence Jesus said, "So, you have kept God's commandments? How about the one that says 'You shall have no other gods before me'? Let's see how free you are from the love of *things*." To prove his point, he instructed the young man to sell his goods, give the proceeds to the poor, and become a disciple.

He loved the man enough to expose how love of power and possessions was keeping him from God, from heaven. Jesus loved him enough to offer himself as the man's teacher and savior. But Mr. Ruler quietly walked away dejected. He became a picture of everyone who is consumed by himself, everyone who has rejected real love.

## LOVE REJECTED

What a disaster! Consider the consequences of rejecting divine love in the story.

**First, to reject God's love is to reject truth:** Mr. Ruler stopped hearing the voice of God. His heart was hardened. No way would he listen to such radical and ridiculous instructions! It would mean handing over all he had worked for to others who refused to lift an undeserving finger! Mr. Ruler would not be humiliated, would not be known as the fool who gave it all away. By this stubbornness, he spiritually drowned out Jesus' voice, with earbuds streaming only the sounds of his own podcast.

**Second, to reject God's love ends hope:** Mr. Ruler had brimmed with expectancy. This encounter was supposed to resolve his most gnawing problem but he turned away without the anticipated relief. Now, his future was bleak. Stunned. Confused perhaps? Is it possible that Jesus was a poor choice? What could be more tragic than to leave the presence of God in despair.

Having rejected Jesus' confrontational but life-giving love, Mr. Ruler left deflated, disappointed, and without a future. There would be no quick fix. Jesus had showed this man real love. He did this by revealing the man's idols, demanding that he part with them, and offering to be his Master. In so speaking, Jesus was not teaching that salvation is earned by commandment-keeping. He was teaching the need for everyone — for the ruler, for you, for me — to see sin for what it really is, to see the depth of its offense. No one can travel two roads at the same time. No one can please two masters. We must love the one and forsake the other. But the rich young ruler clung to his work and to what it bought — at the cost of eternity.

There is nothing like being loved by Jesus. He did not just *claim* to love us. He proved it by leaving heaven for this sad planet and dying a horrific death for us who despised him. When we reflect on our lives, what do we see? If we cherish ourselves or the things of this life more than Jesus, we forfeit unspeakable love.

## LOVE IN **WASHINGTON**

For much of the world, Washington is all about power, personalities, and favorable policies. What a novelty it would be if the Rome of today's world were a place where one could find love in the midst of rule! To be a city that truly serves people, it would have to be a city of love. Not the self-love of Instagram or that which Robert Gates mocked, but the love of others that comes only from having accepted the confrontational but life-giving love of Jesus. For us to have that love, we need to know Jesus — to grasp who he is, what he has done for us, and to embrace the implications for how we think, speak, and behave. Only then can we be *in* Washington without being *of* Washington.

# ACKNOWLEDGEMENTS

The gospel means everything to me. Properly expressing its message to the world in which I live is a great challenge. I deeply appreciate the help which has been provided through kind and patient friends over the last of couple years. Barbara Harley, a long time Oklahoma writing mentor, graciously edited this manuscript. Her insights, counsel and countless hours of discourse transformed my writing. I cannot say enough of the timely wisdom directed to me from Steve Estes who in many ways made a better book. Former team member Will Clark, at present a Master of Divinity student in the Northeast, provided needed advice. Amy Stoller's thoughtful critiques came at just the right time. And, just before I was finished, John Moolenaar gave helpful insights as we sat outside the US House chambers on a cold

December day. Gleaning from his years in politics removed some of the remaining rough edges.

There are others who invested in this writing project for which I am indebted. My children and their spouses, Philip, Brooke, Tony, Katie, Anna and Peter always have important views, graciously shared.

And last of all, I am very thankful to my wife Debby who patiently encourages me through the entire process. Her chapter reviews are priceless.

# END NOTES

## CHAPTER 1 **PRESENCE**

1. Alfred Edersheim, *Sketches of Jewish Social Life*, (Peabody, Hendrickson Publishers, 1994), 30-41.

## CHAPTER 2 **OFFENSE**

2. Anne Frank, the Dutch girl known for her diary written while in hiding from the Nazis, penned the following:

"It's a wonder I haven't abandoned all my ideals, they seem so absurd and impractical. Yet I cling to them because I still believe, in spite of everything, that people are truly good at heart. It's utterly impossible for me to build my life on a foundation of chaos, suffering and death. I see the world being slowly transformed into a wilderness, I hear the approaching thunder that, one day, will destroy us too, I feel the suffering of millions. And yet, when I look up at the sky, I somehow feel that everything will change for the better, that this cruelty too shall end, that peace and tranquility will return once more."

*Friday- July 15, 1944,* The Diary of a Young Girl, Anne Frank, (*The Annex: Diary Notes 14 June 1942 – 1 August 1944,* Contact Publishing, Amsterdam,1947).
How often we hear a governor or president claim similarly, "I believe in the basic goodness of the American people." Any suggestion to the contrary offends greatly.
If people are basically good why carry all the keys and ask for security codes and pin numbers that need constant updating? Why security cameras? What need is there for safe deposit boxes? Why all the laws backed up with a complex judicial system that includes police and prisons? Why do both the US Senate and House have ethics committees and armed capitol police?

## CHAPTER 3 **COST**

3.  J. I. Packer, *Knowing God,* (Downers Grove: Inter Varsity Press, 1973), 148-157.

4.  J. I. Packer, *Knowing God,* 150.

## CHAPTER 4 **HUMILITY**

5.  Peter Jamison, "D. C. homeless population drops for second straight year, report finds,"(Washington, D.C., Washington Post,2016), https://www.washingtonpost.com/local/dc-politics/dc-homeless-population-drops-for-second-straight-year-report-finds/2018/05/08/5505b828-5238-11e8-abd8-265bd07a9859_story.html?noredirect=on&utm_term=.62d42a5f9658, (accessed 2018).

## CHAPTER 5 **POWER**

6.  "How Deep is the Ocean", National Oceanic and Atmospheric Administration, https://oceanservice.noaa.gov/facts/oceandepth.html, (accessed 2018).

7.   "How Big is Our Universe?", NASA, https://www.nasa.gov/audience/
     foreducators/5-8/features/F_How_Big_is_Our_Universe.html,
     (accessed 2018).

## CHAPTER 6 DEATH

8.   C. S. Lewis, *The Screwtape Letters*, (New York: HarperCollins
     Publishers,1996).

## CHAPTER 7 FASHION

9.   "Bosnia-Herzegovina," United States Holocaust Memorial Museum,
     https://www.ushmm.org/confront-genocide/cases/bosnia-herzegovina,
     (accessed 2018).

10.  Eline Gordts, "5 Staggering Statistics For Why We Can Never
     Let A Tragedy Like Rwanda's Happen Ever Again," Huffington
     Post, https://www.huffingtonpost.com/2014/04/06/rwanda-
     genocide_n_5084747.html, (accessed 2018).

11.  Paul Johnson, *Modern Times*, (New York, Harper and Row, Publishers,
     1991) 783.

12.  "Poverty headcount ratio at $1.90 a day," https://data.worldbank.org/
     indicator/SI.POV.DDAY, (accessed 2018).

13.  David Paul Tripp, *Parenting: 14 Gospel Principles That Can Radically
     Change Your Family*, (Wheaton, Crossway, 2016), 26.

14.  J. Gresham Machen, *Christianity and Liberalism*, (Grand Rapids,
     William B. Eerdmans Publishing Company, 1923).

## CHAPTER 8 INFLUENCE

15.  Garth Lean, *God's Politician*, (Colorado Springs: Helmers & Howard
     Publishers,1987).

16. C. F. Keil, *Biblical Commentary on the Book of Daniel,* (Grand Rapids, William B. Eerdmans Publishing Company, 1980), 80.

17. Edward J. Young, *The Prophecy of Daniel,* (Grand Rapids, William B. Eerdmans Publishing Company,1949), 44.

## CHAPTER 9 LEADERSHIP

18. Paul Johnson, *A History of the Jews,* (New York, Harper and Row, Publishers, 1987), 54.

## CHAPTER 10 REST

19. William Manchester and Paul Reid, *The Last Lion,* (New York, Bantam Books, 2013), 462,463.

## CHAPTER 11 LOVE

20. Robert Gates, "Secretary of Defense Speech", http://archive.defense.gov/speeches/speech.aspx?speechid=1467, (accessed 2018).

# ABOUT THE
# AUTHOR

Charles Garriott was born in Baltimore, Maryland, and educated at the University of Baltimore and Covenant Theological Seminary. For over twenty years he pastored in Oklahoma City. He develops ministry to those in government in Washington, D.C., as well as other state and international capitals, under the auspices of Mission to North America, Presbyterian Church in America. He has authored *Work Excellence: A Biblical Perspective of Work; Obama Prayer: Prayers for the 44th President; Rulers: Gospel and Government,* and *Prayers for Trump: Petitions for the 45th President.* He lives with his wife Debby in the District of Columbia. They have four children and seven grandchildren.

# STUDY GUIDE/
## SMALL GROUPS

A website has been established to provide
additional content and conversation.

Study guide questions for small groups
and blog posts are included.

Reduced prices for bulk orders of *Love and
Power: Glimpses of the Gospel for those Addicted to
Self* may be obtained from the same website.

www.loveandpowerbook.com